She Presents Well

Kenneth J. Smith

Strategic Book Publishing and Rights Co.

Strategic Book Publishing and Rights Co.
12620 FM 1960, Suite A4-507
Houston, TX 77065
www.sbpra.com

ISBN: 978-1-62516-956-3

Design: Dedicated Book Services (www.netdbs.com)

Dedication

This book is dedicated to my grandmothers

Madeline Schmitt Ryan (1905-1991)

and

Jennie Fisher Smith (1889-1980)

May they rest in peace after long journeys through the darkness of dementia.

Table of Contents

Chapter 1: Who Lives Here

Petronella

I don't really know how I can just be standing by the sink one moment and the next thing I know, I am flat on my ass with my chin nuzzling the base of the toilet. I am in excruciating pain. My hip is broken? My hip is definitely broken! They say you don't break your hip and fall, rather, as you are falling, it's breaking on the way down toward the cold bathroom floor.

Anyway, every time I have to pee at night, I think nothing of swinging my legs off the side of the bed—there are no side rails yet, thank God—and landing on them to walk the three steps to that dingy little john I share with three other ladies. Well, you can surely guess what happens next. The same fall that landed me in the hospital, and eventually here, simply reoccurs and reoccurs. So, I have a new label taped on the wall above my headboard. They call me a "fall risk." And my name—I do still have one, you know—is on the falls risk prevention workgroup's list of "fallers." How do I know? Because Ermine, my weekday CNA, told me. That's a Certified Nursing Assistant. They run the joint. Really, I'm not kidding, they do. Well, sort of, anyway.

You are well aware that we are not supposed to hear these things about us or actually be part of the process. The other day, Ermine was wiping my butt and Joanne was feeding

Betty, in the bed next to me. Ermine was telling Joanne that I fell again and they have me on the list of frequent fallers. Clever name, huh? So she has to check on me more frequently, and soon the nurses are putting me on a bed alarm. I feel I'm becoming just like some animal. They'll tuck the alarm under my sheet and it will sound when I dare to move from it, presumably to take my little three-step walk to pee.

Don't even get me started about when the batteries die, don't get replaced, we fall anyway, and get blamed for it because our meds aren't "responding well to our diagnosis," whatever the hell that means!

I miss my freedom, and I miss my dignity. I miss my crappy little apartment on West Third in Southie. I miss the nice little drunken Irish lady that used to be my homemaker. She kept me safe. No one at the Boston Medical Center asked me how or where I wanted to recover from my broken hip episode. I'm just suddenly here. Some time passes and I am suddenly living here two years. How did it happen? But, more importantly, why did it happen? Where was I when it was happening? I distinctly remember telling someone I didn't want to be here and wanted to get back home. I thought that person heard me. Was it *that* social worker? I swear, I just cannot remember, but why wasn't I consulted? Why didn't they listen to me? I am so sorry for this rant, but I cannot take another day of this—this institution with their crappy food, people screaming at me as if I am deaf, and this sharing of a little eight-by-eight room with a stranger who dribbles her baby food as they shove it into her mouth with a spoon. I can't stand living like this, and more than anything, watching the dying. I want my voice back. I want them to hear my thoughts, hear what I am saying . . . to you now.

I want to understand what I did in life to be subjected to these indecencies. Why do a series of strange girls—strange to me anyway—put diapers on me and clean my privates after I've messed myself again? Why? Oh, please don't look at my tears. I cannot stand pity or another moment of feeling inadequate, invisible, decrepit, and useless. What about you, how are you feeling about living here?

Mary

Well you know, Petz, I was brought here against my will. There was no fall and no layover at a hospital. My daughter-in-law called the cops on me. Yes, I am telling you the truth. I was living in my house in Jamaica Plain and apparently left the gas stove on once or twice. It could have been more, but really who's counting? As if I *wouldn't* have noticed the smell of gas eventually. I just can't see the strict correlation between a stove left on and having to be sent here. I know I can live at home alone and I *am* going to get back there. I have called the Attorney General's office, the Ombudsman, the Department of Public Health, and that nice Senator from my district. They are *all* going to help me get out of this place. I am going mad and absolutely have to get back home. I DON'T BELONG

HERE! Sorry for screaming, Petz, but I am not like the rest of these people here; they're all mad as hatters. I know everything that's going on around me, and they can't fool me with all this talk about dementia and Alzheimer's type dementia, as they call it. I am not crazy and will not be told that I am!

At least some of my CNAs know I am not crazy, or at the very least, that I can retain enough information to tell a nurse a few minutes later how I was treated. Of course, I am not on the other end when the nurse questions the CNA, who may very well retort that she *never treated Mary like that, nor would she ever do anything but be perfectly gentle with the poor, dear, elderly patients.* God! Now I am crazy, old, *and poor.* How did this happen to me? Where was I when it was starting to happen? Unless I come down here to chat with you, I am just looking out that same window day after day, just peering out at nothing, hoping and hoping this nightmare will come to an end and I will be back in my cozy little home on the parkway in Jamaica Plain. I'm third generation JP, and I was going to stay in that house until I died.

But, that daughter-in-law of mine . . . well, I am sure it was jealousy. She was jealous of my relationship with Richard—my son, her husband. A mother can't *love her son?* She can't hold onto *that* love? I just don't understand what happened. I also think it was my mink. Sharon knew I had the mink and her greedy little cat eyes saw dollar signs, and she was not going to let me enjoy any money she thought I had. So, you might ask, why would she send me here, where I burned through all my money to the tune of about eight thousand dollars per month? It's a good question. I suppose they could have hidden my assets and signed my house over so this stinking nursing home couldn't get my money. Maybe that's what happened to my home. I just want to be back there since I know I don't belong here!

"Care Plan." That's a real laugh. If Sharon and Richard care so much about me, where are they when this place holds a meeting every three months to talk about my so-called care? As if this place even needs to plan for my care. They bring that tray in with the so-called food three times a day, ply me with gobs of pills at least four times a day that I can recall, and tell me to be sure to use my walker or I'll fall.

Apparently I am one of a few people of the 121 here who actually goes to this so-called care plan meeting. I insist I should be there if they are talking about me. But lo and behold, when I focus—OK, passionately focus—on getting out of here, I am told that such disruptive behavior will bar me from future meetings. As I leave in a huff, I hear the nurse and social worker say in hushed tones that, "Mary's dementia is progressing rapidly, causing these 'behaviors,' and she really shouldn't be coming to these care plan meetings anyway." Hmmmf, is what I say to that attitude.

Bertha

I am the luckiest woman alive. These doctors and nurses are taking such wonderful care of me that I just couldn't imagine a better place to be. Everyone is so sweet and kind. And that poor, sweet, debilitated woman next to me is just such a gift. I do truly believe God brought me here to help take care of Dorothy. When I *do* go home, I intend to come back every day to help Dorothy in any way I can. She just cries out every few minutes not even knowing what she needs or to whom she is reaching out. I think she has the Oltimers disease. I think that's what they call it. It is just so devastating to watch, but let me tell you, those daughters of hers are here every day. They take turns—Jackie during the day and Caroline in the evenings. I let them both know there is no need to worry because I am here. I talk to Dorothy. I let her know I'm here. But the CNA girls here are just fabulous, and I don't think they give Dorothy any special attention just because she's also black or because her daughters are here so much. I've heard that talk from families that if the girls see families here often, they provide better care to those patients. I simply don't believe that. I know these girls here care about everyone equally—they are not paying a bit of attention to who has visitors and who does not. Jackie says her mother gets changed only if she runs out to the nurses' station and announces her mother has soiled her pants. This just isn't true. I have seen the girls stop in and check on Dorothy at least every fifteen minutes. When the people from the state come here each year to evaluate the home and the staff, I tell them all about how the girls check on Dorothy all the time. They seem so happy to hear that!

Once Jackie found a dirty diaper under the bed. I thought she was going to die until I explained that I was helping with Dorothy one night and I dropped it there because it was late and I didn't want to turn the light on and disturb our neighbors across the hall.

Eve handles so much I just couldn't bear to expose her to Dorothy's daughters when they're angry. Eve is what they call the unit manager. She's in charge of this part of the home—the fourth floor. She talks to all the families when they are complaining, works with the doctors, the other patients, and most importantly, the administration. She keeps them posted on everything they need to know about us. It's such a wonderful system—they are running this intricate business and letting us all feel like it's our home. And it is, you know, for so many of these people. They just couldn't live in their own homes anymore. I can and will again, but until this leg heals, I am thrilled with being a patient here. I am going to recommend all my friends and neighbors come here when they come down with a leg ulcer.

Michael

Multiple sclerosis? I am too young and the wrong sex. Isn't this a disease for women in their fifties? I'm sixty years old. This isn't fair.

"You won't see any symptoms for at least five to ten years. And it's a very slow progression, allowing you to live a very normal life." Normal? It has been anything but normal. At forty-two, I moved to this place. My sixty-three-year-old mother and sixty-nine-year-old father couldn't lift me and drag me up the thirteen stairs to my bedroom. And once I couldn't get to the bathroom on time, wiping the ass of your forty-one-year-old son wasn't what either of them bargained for. So, they stuck me here. Was it the best option? Don't know, could have been. It's basically hell on earth, but I try not to mention that to Dad. He's eighty-seven now and still comes every day. She died two years ago, but he still takes my laundry home twice each week. Doesn't matter at all to him that the nursing home does all of the other patients' laundry. What matters to Dad is that he has never forgiven himself for dumping me here. I've forgiven him completely, though. There was no way he could have continued to cart around a six-foot-two, 220-pound son. I tell him how shitty the food is and how the nurses and CNAs don't really respect me because I'm not elderly, but I have never done anything to make him feel guilty. That wouldn't be fair to the old man, would it? But it is guilt. For putting me here, for not keeping me at home, for not trying harder, for not understanding MS, for what I really don't know. I know I don't try to make him feel guilty. No one does that to their loved one just because that loved one warehoused them in a shit-hole like this.

Dad was here last night screaming at the nurse about my underwear continually being filled with feces. They offered to do my laundry here, but he insisted on taking it home. They offered to put me in adult diapers, but he refused. He wants me to be proud and wear underwear like any other middle-aged man. He wants me to be treated better than all the oldsters here. This thought, coming from an eighty-something-year-old. What *is* so terrible about this place from his perspective anyway? He doesn't have to stay awake each night listening to those screams, the neighbor falling on her way to the bathroom, the cry—that wretched cry as she falls and her hip cracks on the way down. I can hear it. I can hear the death rattle when one is leaving us. It's painful—their hollowness, their despair, and their slow descent into nothingness, through a noisy, godforsaken garble. At least that's what we see. Those "lucky" enough not to lose it. It's this inevitable hurricane that encircles their speech, their mobility, their brain. I often wonder, is anyone watching or paying attention? Does anyone keep track of the descent? Does anyone wonder what they're thinking, what thoughts go through their minds, if sentences still form in their brains when they sit there staring blankly at their daughter or son?

There is a hint of the former self. Do you see it? I do. It's when they speak incessantly with one another or to themselves. You can hear it, some recollection from her past. In perfect locution, she will tell you the story about her high school graduation and the rose she carried, how her parents were there. She never saw her mother smile so much until and since that day. Lena's father told her that day about his dream when he was arriving in Boston's North End from Italy. He dreamed of setting up a shop and selling fresh fish

from the Atlantic. He dreamed of giving his children everything he never had and, more important than anything, above
all else, he wanted to see his daughter Lena graduate from
secondary school. That day clearly struck a chord for her.
She can still tell the story in exact clarity, like that summer's
day her mind once resembled.

Chapter 2: She Presents Well

Sally Cournan joined the social work team last week. After many years serving in an internship with people with severe intellectual disabilities and another eight years discharge-planning for the care of young men and women with spinal cord injuries, she was more than ready for a break. That's what *she* thought. They hired Sally without the benefit of her ever having worked in a nursing home before, but she had the right initials after her name, MSW, Master of Social Work. As long as she had that master's degree, she was ready to manage all the problems of a population that consisted primarily of folks with dementia and Alzheimer's, with a little multiple sclerosis in the mix. She had solid experience counseling adults with disabilities and working with them to determine the best set of services for living independently at home. The only difference with this population was their age and the fact they were already home with little chance of parole.

Sally commenced official duties with a tour of the 160-bed facility, and for 120 of the beds she would be the only social worker. She walked the cold and lonely halls for hours and hours on that gray Monday morning. She popped her head into the rooms where one or two ladies were inside and not lined up outside the room along the handrail. Sally thought they lined up as if a parade were about to pass. The ladies watched a parade of nurses, nurse's aides, rehab aides, and laundry and housekeeping employees go by all day long, but this might not have been the parade they had in mind.

Sally entered these little rooms in hopes of getting to know her new population. No one had explained that so many of her 120 would be languishing in bed or slumped over in wheelchairs. Approaching one of them, trying to ignore the overpowering urine and fecal odors, Sally said a timid, "How are you, Mrs. Lavoie?" No response except a very blank stare. A sad, blank, lonely stare. No matter how zonked out the people looked, her immediate thought was, *Just how over-medicated do we have these poor people?*

"Mrs. Lavoie, can you hear me?" Her volume now rising, she would say, "My name is Sally Cournan. I'm the new social worker here at St. Matthew, your home." It hadn't yet occurred to Sally that this might not be what Cecelia Lavoie had ever considered her home. Cecelia's eyeballs *did* move or rolled in a counterclockwise direction.

"I'll be back when you're feeling better," Sally promised her.

After fourteen or fifteen similar interactions, Sally switched her focus to the residents lined up in the hallways. She had a few limited conversations where she asked each person how they were doing, receiving many "Fine," "OK," or "I'm good" responses. As she passed the nurses' station, one nurse was on the phone with a pharmacy, another nurse was writing furiously on a chart, and a third was heading to the medicine cart with additional supplies.

"I'm Florence, you must be the new social worker."

"I am. How did you know?" Sally asked.

"You all look alike. Anyway, hon, do you know what you're doing? I mean, you look the part, but you're talking to them like you're gonna get an answer. I've been here eighteen years, and this is what you get. It's actually worse every year, seeing as how they stay at home as long as possible before giving up. Or, before the yuppie daughter dumps her here because she doesn't want to pay for adult day care between 3:30 and 8 p.m. I mean, how can she possibly leave her high-powered job at 4 or 5 p.m. and, God forbid, come right home? Some know they're being dumped here, others are, thankfully, already clueless. Sad state we're in, Sandy."

"It's Sally, but I hadn't introduced myself yet."

"Hon, it's on your name tag you've pinned on your sweater."

Pulling her state-mandated name tag off her blouse, Sally noted that indeed she was typed up as "Sandy Cournan."

"I'll give you a tour. It will help you to familiarize yourself with the place and know who's who. If you have time, I'll tell you about the family members to avoid and which ones support us. And which residents watch our every step and which ones are so demented they have no idea."

"Do you really think that's the appropriate way to refer to the individuals we serve?"

"You really did just fall off the college truck, didn't you?"

Sally quickly retorted, "No, I've been practicing social work in health care settings for over twenty years."

"Don't get your panties in a bunch. I'm just saying . . . So, this is Rita Cranston." Flo spoke in a hushed tone. "Rita is one of our favorites. Aren't you, Rita?"

"Oh, hi, honey." Rita was definitely what Sally had in mind when she took this job. "Now, who is our new friend here?"

Flo leaned in and said, "Rita, this is Sally Cournan, our new social worker."

Rita looked concerned and happy at the same time. She had been through a number of social workers in her five years here. She wasn't sure she was ready to break in another one. She tried to remember the name Flo had just said, but deflected instead.

"So, welcome aboard. I'm sure you'll love it here. I'll show you around and ensure that you know who's who and who to ignore. Some of these old girls don't really know what they are talking about anymore, and I'll keep you straight on all of that. Now, you know we will have to discuss the night shift and weekends. There is simply not enough supervision. And there's no management around and the CNAs run amok. The call bells go unanswered. And some of these old girls just sit in their muck for hours. Also, there just aren't enough staff on weekends. I am so glad that you are, I'm assuming, here to fix all of that."

Sally asked, "Do the administrator and director of nursing know about these issues?"

"Oh sure, I've told them. So they know. They each come for a couple of hours on a Saturday about once a month or less. So things change for a few hours, but they all start swinging from the chandeliers in no time after they've left."

Sally gasped, "Oh, it couldn't be that bad, Rita."

"You'll see."

"Rita, tell me a little more about you. I'm especially curious about your choice to come here. Also, are you part of the Resident Council?"

"Of course I am. But no one really listens at those meetings. Most just gripe incoherently for hours, and that crazy Bertha just carries on about how wonderful everyone and everything is. Boy, is she on another planet. Then, Michael starts in with his boorish behavior and vulgar language. He hates the food. So, what else is new? We've heard it all before. You'll see. We'll invite you to the next council meeting."

Later that day Sally met with her supervisor, Joan Morgan, to discuss her first day and her goals for the people on her caseload.

Joan began the discussion, "What did you think?"

"I wasn't expecting so many people with such advanced dementia, or, that so few have hardly any cognitive deficits at all, for that matter," Sally said.

"What did you think you'd encounter here? If they weren't advanced they wouldn't be here yet. Sally, people stay at home as long as possible now. If they need care, they go to an assisted living facility for as long as possible. This place is their last resort. Don't you see? And by the way, those you think have no dementia yet, they just present well."

"It's just that I love to counsel. There's not too many peo-ple I can spend time counseling. How can I even work on solving their problems if they can't even tell me what's on their minds?"

"Counsel, really? Wasn't I clear in the interview? I am so sorry I didn't explain better what's involved here. It's the families you'll be working with primarily. You'll deal with their complaints about missing laundry, the room being too cramped or not clean enough. This is huge. More impor-tantly, you'll deal with their undying, perennial family guilt and how it manifests itself."

Sally interjected, "How *does* it manifest itself?"

"That's the fun part. The families will let you know about every single issue and problem with this place that is real or imagined. You'll hear about the fan in the bathroom not working properly, all the way to our aides not wiping their mother well enough after a bowel movement. We also hear an awful lot about the food not being up to par or the way mom used to cook, as well as the numerous complaints about the missing or mangled laundry items."

"So, it's all about, 'Since we can't do it for her, it will never be as good as if we did keep her at home.'"

"Bingo, Sal!"

"So, I got to meet Rita today. She is so with-it. Other than using a wheelchair, it just doesn't seem right that she's al-ready here. I don't understand why she isn't getting home care according to what you said."

"She presents well."

"What?"

"Sally, Rita has dementia like almost every other resident here. She isn't 'with-it,' she merely *presents* well. Her mind has enough left to know how to try hard and trick us 'with-it' folks."

"She presents well? It seems more than that. I mean, she seems more than just that phrase."

"She's not, Sally. She's not."

Sally was in for a rude awakening. She wanted these new clients to be malleable and able to be helped. The more she stuck around, the more she saw there wasn't much to do in the way of social work as she had always known it. She was determined, however, to find a way to help them. It must just be a different kind of help they needed. She needed to *be needed.*

Chapter 3: The Courtyard

Sally started making her rounds the next day. As she did, she noticed that every day the residents were taken in their wheelchairs to a solarium type room affectionately known as "The Courtyard." It resembled a real solarium in the winter and actually became one in the summer, when the sliders were opened to the real world somewhere out there.

The residents were placed in a circle in hopes of enhancing their dialogue with one another. Some just stared off blankly while others simply looked ahead and drooled. Then there was Connie's mantra, "Safe and sound, God bless us all, safe and sound, God bless us all." This cry continued for hours every day, even during the so-called *social* hours in the courtyard. Occasionally, annoyance registered with someone who yelled back at Connie, "Shut up, you!" Connie's retort to that was, "Safe and sound, God bless us all."

Looking around the room, Sally saw a circle of something that had the appearance of normalcy but yielded nothing more than utter sadness. It was a group of about nine people looking broken and making little sense when they spoke. It was unclear whether they perceived each other as making sense or not. Sally wondered, *What does transpire in their minds? What are they thinking about, themselves or each other? And those not in wheelchairs are looking at them and talking at them? Do they think they've died, or is it more that they feel trapped in a body that doesn't move and lips that*

*won't form the sentences their brains are trying to formu-
late?* The most common thought on this topic, as Sally understood it, was that the person no longer has any idea where
they are, who they are, and what surroundings they are in.
Others in the field were not so convinced of that.

Sally noticed someone she hadn't met yet in her first few
days on the job. She approached her and saw that her nursing
home-issued wristband read "Doris."

Doris

Doris was now catatonic. Doris's dementia progressed relatively slowly while she was still living at home with her husband, after the children were grown and gone. Slowly at first,
then suddenly, more often than not when Stanley came home
from work, dinner went from not being on the table to not even
on the stove. Then, Stanley came home from work one day to
the distinct odor of feces. Doris was sitting in the living room,
and as it turns out, forgot to walk to the bathroom a few hours
earlier.

Doris and Stanley's daughter, Jessica, took her to the hospital after bartering with many other waitresses at the local
diner to take off that particular lunch shift. Stanley worked
that day. Jessica heard something like, "vascular dementia
or frontal lobe, not Alzheimer's, but similar, they are related
anyway, Alzheimer's being one type of dementia." Head spinning, Jessica asked the good doctor if the bowel movement

accident issue would happen again. At this point, the doctor realized she wasn't explaining everything to Jessica as well as she could have.

Dr. Susan Cloutier asked Jessica to sit down for a few minutes if she had the time. Jessica soon got a crash course in how dementia would capture and take hold of her mother's mind, possibly her legs, her arms, and even her soul. The doctor spouted off options and ideas for caretaking despite seeing that Jessica had not grabbed a pen from her pocketbook. The family can be numb like that at such times. This, Jessica would later realize, was one of many funerals she would attend for her mother. The real one—further down the line—would not compare to the hell and succession of funerals she will be attending.

So, Stanley and Jessica tried using visiting nurses and home health care aides for a few months. Insurance covers the home health care aide for only about an hour each day. They learned that even that is a relatively short-term arrangement. Stanley began paying privately for an aide to work extra hours when it became increasingly apparent Doris couldn't be in the house on her own. Jessica scaled back her shifts at the restaurant; Stanley tried to leave work early a couple of days each week to piece together a patchwork of "adult-sitting." Jessica did not like when Stanley called it "babysitting." She would argue with her father that, "just because Ma is losing her ability to speak and control her bodily functions, it doesn't make her a baby." Sally would soon be wishing, "If only everyone thought this much about restoring some dignity to people in Doris's shoes."

Soon enough, Doris called the health care aides "Jessica" and called her daughter by their names. This was followed by accusing the aides of stealing her jewelry—which was all still in the jewelry box—and the inevitable yelling at them to get out of her house and stop trying to strip her naked and put her in that awful contraption, the bathtub. Taking a bath when one has dementia is not a happy or welcoming experience.

What happened next, of course, is that Stanley and Jessica went nursing home shopping. This was not a fun experience either. They spent a few nights and an entire weekend once trying to see seven nursing homes in the surrounding towns. Most looked pretty nice, but they were seldom shown anything above the first floor. In one home, staff actually corrected them about the name, explaining that "these buildings are now called a nursing facility," which certainly didn't seem very nice or homey, but Stanley and Jessica went with the flow. Jessica thought the tour guide, aptly named "Admissions Director," was trying to avoid them being hit head-on with the odor of bodily fluids. Little did she know that this had become a reality in Stanley and Jessica's lives already. While a couple of these "nursing facilities" seemed relatively nice, both Stanley and Jessica had a gnawing feeling about sending Doris to live in one of these places. *How do you sleep the first few nights after putting your parent in a nursing home?* Jessica wondered.

The afternoon they brought Doris, she carried a suitcase with two nightgowns, a few pairs of underpants, a couple of bras, a Bible, a sweater, a few pairs of slacks, blouses, and a carton of Depends. Doris believed she was going to a hospital for a few nights stay. She thought it was awfully sweet when she found a picture of Stanley and her from the cruise they took to Bermuda back in 1985. *Stanley didn't want me to miss him while I'm in the hospital,* Doris thought. Unknown to her, he didn't want her to miss him while she got used to living in her new home.

The room was about as big as her husband's den back home, but this narrow rectangle with four walls was inhabited by two single beds, two little three-drawer bureaus, and two nightstands. The other patient, as Doris thought of her, didn't seem to leave her bed. As if they were just dropped off at the county jail, Doris asked Thelma, "What are you in for?" She expected an answer or something that resembled an answer, but perhaps Doris didn't know what to expect anymore, considering she wasn't sure how she was answering people anymore when they asked her questions. Either way, Thelma didn't answer but made a noise that came out as something like a groan. Doris thought she must be really sick. She must be here for an operation.

So, Doris now had a new home. Every morning she asked whomever would listen, "Where am I?" She looked at the picture on her "hospital" nightstand and was reminded of the man she married. She picked up the phone to ask Stanley when she was going home and when he was visiting, as she assumed her operation must be over by now. She couldn't get past the first three numbers—the 873. They weren't even the right three, as Doris wasn't remembering the area-code-first dialing.

"Help, help! I need help dialing my husband."

No one came at first, since Doris forgot about the cord she was instructed to pull that sets off a blink and a beep at the nurses' station. About fifteen minutes later, one of the CNAs was walking by and heard the cry for help.

"Doris, honey, what's wrong?"

Doris asked, "How do you know my name?"

"Well, honey, I've known your name since you came in last month. I help you bathe every day and change you most days too. In fact, you're one of my favorite residents. I'm Lea. You remember me, don't you, Doris?" Clearly, Lea had forgotten what she learned at the recent in-service about how to mitigate confusion and disorientation when a demented individual is especially lost and confused.

"What does 'change me' mean?" Doris continued. "And I *am* just visiting. I'm going home soon, so I'm a resident of *what*?" Her voice steadily rising, she repeated who, when, and where over and over, until it reached a crescendo sounding like," Whyyyyyyyyy?"

When Sally came upon this scene and did some preliminary investigating, she asked herself, *What is the unfortunate question? What is Doris asking about?* Obviously, she is trying to ask why she is here; or, is it why is she not at home, or better yet, why is she unclear about where she is or who she is or why she is confused? Oh, the beautifully sad world of Alzheimer's! Sally didn't know whether to cry or run screaming.

Doris often asked herself "what"— what is this place, what is this state of mind, what is Stanley doing right now, what is he thinking, does he know what I'm doing or what I am thinking, or what happened to my thinking? It became a cyclical thought pattern whirling in her head like the eye of a tornado.

The days continued blurring into months and years and, concurrently, Doris's mind continued to blur with past thoughts and disconnections causing her mind to sizzle, fade in and out and then in again, like the makeshift antenna on a transistor radio. The nursing staff placed Doris in her wheel-chair against the wall that faces the nurses' station on the unit. This was a recent development caused by her mind no longer telling her body how to perform and function. There she would sit among five or six fellow residents in a row, in chairs that allowed the inevitable atrophy of their legs coin-ciding with their minds' descent into nowhere. She sat next to Michael, Cecelia, George, Joan, and Olivia, and some-times Bertha joined.

There they sat and stared and occasionally blurted some-thing out. It usually lacked sense, but other times it was a clear thought or even a request. "I need to go." "Where am

I?" "When are we going to eat?" "Where's my husband?" "Don't make me take that." "Please, not again." "How are you?" The phrases were repeatedly spoken to anyone who walked by. These came from some of the group, but almost all of them said something from time to time. Except Doris. Over the past year, Doris had gradually lost her speech. She stopped commenting on food, medicine, and sadly stopped asking why, what, where, and when.

In the beginning, Stanley brought Doris home for the day on Sundays. If Jessica had the day off from work and family obligations allowed, she would join in seeing Doris at her home. Wednesday would have been the chosen day for a home visit if Jessica had her way. But Stanley wanted things to be the same with him and Doris, as they had been for over fifty years of marriage. He liked to remember that feeling or sense of the good old days before her mind was ravaged by this strangely named disease. When planting Doris in the kitchen and asking her to make supper yielded nothing, when motioning to the laundry room brought no hint of recollection, they simply resumed their positions in the living room in their Edith and Archie chairs. After a while, Stanley no longer saw any sense in attempting to watch a basketball game with Doris, considering she never liked the sport anyway. It never was their joint routine. So he walked her to their bedroom and told her to get undressed. Doris asked if it was bedtime already and wasn't sure if she had eaten dinner yet. He explained little and acted on his impulses more.

After the first Sunday visit, the nurses noticed something different about Doris and thought she didn't look too keen and a bit pale, possibly a little more confused than usual. The following Sunday she sputtered and repeated, "Please don't make me!" but still the nurses on duty made no connection. As time passed, Doris came back saying less, moving more gingerly, and more and more tired to the point of looking exhausted.

Two months ago, Corrine was the nurse on the evening shift the night Jessica returned her mother and demanded to see the medication list, as she was certain her mother must be over-medicated. Jessica told Corrine her mother seemed more lethargic, spoke less and less, and seemed on the verge of a catatonic state. Corrine handled the situation pretty well. She explained that the attending physician assigned to Doris pre-scribed medication and signed off on every new medication. She also took time to explain which diagnosis each medicine was prescribed for and the possible side effects of each. Jessica was grateful, but still not comprehending the disease or the fact it inhabited her mother like a cancerous tumor.

"A catatonic state" was a pretty accurate description, and Doris had been slipping into it for some time. That evening, Marie St. Jean, the CNA assigned to Doris, prepared her for bed. When changing her Depends, she immediately noticed blood mixed with her urine and a third fluid that could have been puss, but Marie St. Jean suspected differently. Corrine was called in and a determination was quickly made.

Sally was briefed first thing Monday morning. She tried successfully throughout her career to maintain a dam in her head that suppressed tears, at least until the drive home. This day was different. Sally sobbed quietly with her door closed until she felt foolish, weak, and unprofessional. She picked up the phone and dialed. With Sally's somber tone, Jessica needed to know if her mother had died, and why couldn't Sally just say that over the phone? Sally had to convince her the issue was health-related but that Doris had indeed not expired, and to please just come in at her convenience.

Whether Jessica chose to believe the story or whether she explained to Stanley why there would be no more home visits, Corrine and Sally will never know. But the visits discontinued other than Jessica bringing Doris to her home every Christmas, and not Stanley's. The catatonic state became real and worse.

Joan Morgan had hired a new social worker, Michael Versey, a recent graduate with an MSW from Simmons School of Social Work in Boston. He had been with the nursing home only about a month. Michael got into this field for one reason and one reason only—his absolute love for the elderly and his passion for ensuring their safety and comfort throughout their last days.

Ever since Michael was a child, his fondest memories were of time spent with his grandparents and their tenderness toward him that drew him close. Then, through the cracks in their facade, came the undoing of a lifetime that demonstrated a whole new view for him. He always remembered the times when they made him feel special. Despite any worries they had of their own, Paul and Alice made Michael feel he was the only person in the world when he came to visit them in their little city apartment.

Michael was in his fourth grade classroom at St. Jerome's School when his mother called the principal to request they gather her children to prepare them for an early pick-up. Paul had suffered a fatal heart attack ("hard attack," as Michael had always interpreted the term in his mind) and didn't wake up.

Alice considered herself pretty lucky, and no one quite understood why. It was clear to her, after dealing with her own parents' senility, that this was nothing short of a miracle disguised as a blessing. She was pretty happy Paul wouldn't have to experience any more indignities inherent in growing old. However, Michael's life was forever changed after Paul was lowered into the ground.

Every day since Michael started work at St. Matthew's Nursing Care Center, he walked the corridors trying to wrap his mind around the environment and what was happening there. It was like landing on a desert island and seeing a group of stranded people who can't fend for themselves or even figure out how to get off the island. He didn't know if he was totally unprepared for it or if denial or lack of experience was causing this flood of awakenings. But one thing was clear, he knew that the average Joe has no idea of what we've done to our grandmothers, fathers, aunts, uncles, and especially to our mothers.

Every woman's face could have been Alice and every man's face could have been Paul. Michael just couldn't understand why people were forced to live like this. How did it happen? What was the moment that prompted someone to say, "That's it, Mom's going to Shady Hills today?" What did she say that day as her daughter told her she was being shipped off to a nursing home? What happened to people living at home one day, in their family home, when disease or disability struck? Did the woman scream or cry to elicit such a response and action; or worse, was deception used to get her there? Michael thought to himself that it must be something like "the broken hip syndrome." The elderly person falls, breaks their hip, lands in an acute care hospital, and finally there's the transfer. The transfer is from the hospital to, as the nursing home's marketing team calls it, "The Short-term Rehab Unit."

That night Michael's journal recorded this:

And there they sat. And talked. And reminisced and said something about nothing and nothing about a lot of things; yet, really, they spoke plenty about everything. It was more often what they didn't say that mattered most. The stories that were communicated by peering into each other's souls—through tired, old, sad, and beautiful eyes—were voluminous. Each person could read and interpret what their brain could no longer transmit to their mouth. It was often a subtle read. And other times it came straight from the mouth, or tears, or through anguished cries. How often has the staff heard, "I want to go home . . . Just take me home . . . Get me out of here . . . Where am I? . . . Leave me alone . . . Don't touch me," and, of course, "Who are you?" or "How did I get here?"

These are real. The communication is guttural and pity-inducing, but pointed and honest. They don't know where they are or how they got here, how long they are staying and when they are going home. They aren't really sure what or where home is, but they do know this is not it. It is a perpetual state of unknowingness and loss of centeredness, of a journey to nowhere.

Each person can truly see this in the individual next to them, and it provides her with a sense of empathy. They ban together to create an empathic team or tribe. When Stella cries, "I want to go home," Amanda counters with, "Get me out of here! Take me away!" Pearl, who has moments of lucidity—more than most—upsets the empathy train and informs the group that, "this is your home now." They all move away from Pearl, at least figuratively, if not through staring her down.

Nobody really knows what dementia or the Alzheimer's type of it is, nor do they know that they have it. However, during moments of lucidity, one may get a glimpse into what they know was once normalcy. This takes the shape of a glance in the mirror and recognizing a glint in one's own eye that connects her to the past. Or, peering into the photograph on the nightstand that showcases her beauty and youth. She is smiling and full of confidence, knowing that a world ahead of her offers promise and happiness. That moment takes her by surprise, and she has no idea that an incident is in the making. It's not until she has fallen off her bed, is staring at the ceiling, and Jocelyn, her CNA for the night, asks, "Amanda, what happened to you? Are you all right?" that there is some awareness something has taken her back to a place in time that upset today's clueless state. For a second, anyway.

Michael went back to work the next day determined to pay attention to the world around him. He walked the corridors, looking into each room and its inhabitants. He looked at the nameplate on the wall and then looked into the room to see the faces of Joan and Olivia. He looked at the women curled into fetal positions on their beds, or already propped up in their wheelchairs, or already slumped over to one side. He passed John, who was standing at his toilet trying to urinate through the bars of his walker, a strong odor of spilled urine emanating from his room. Mary was screaming for a cigarette while her CNA was telling her the smoking schedule didn't start until ten o'clock. Lucy screamed from her bed, "Please, somebody help me, help me, help me!" over and over in concise, pathetic repetition.

Michael felt compelled to stop in room 206. It wasn't a conscious decision, rather, it just happened. This may have been the reason he got into this line of work, but if he hadn't stopped, he would have questioned whether he deserved to continue in this work. On some level, he knew—or thought he knew—that she wasn't really in pain; this was nothing her CNA or nurse couldn't tend to. It may have just been that her Depends needed to be changed and someone would get to it sooner or later. But to walk on by with nothing but assumptions as justification for inaction seemed somewhat unconscionable. This was why he took this job, wasn't it?

"Hi, Lucy! What's going on here? Is there anything I can do? Anything you need?" Michael knew he might sound phony and the statement might sound rote, but oh well, it was too late now.

"Help me, help me! I got to get out. I can't stand this bed and this place. I need to go home."

Michael promptly cut in with, "Where do you want to go, Lucy?" Nothing. "Can I call you Lucy?" No disagreement. "Your breakfast is scheduled to come to the room here, but do you prefer to go downstairs to the dining room for breakfast? We can arrange that."

Lucy continued to stare blankly at Michael, without responding to his attempts to engage her.

"Actually, it's eight o'clock and you shouldn't still be in bed. We need to get some help in here to prepare you for this new day." OK, now he *was* sounding a little phony.

"Just get me out of this bed. I've messed myself."

That's all he needed. Flying down the hall, Michael grabbed the first nurse he could and informed her, "Barb, you have to help Lucy. She's had an incontinence episode and has not had a morning care routine. It seems no one has been near her, she's still in bed, and frankly, I think she'll end up with bedsores. And what does she have for family? She talks about going home. Has anyone referred her to Sally? Has Sally spoken with her about this?" He sounded absolutely crazed. His passion for his job and the people who resided here was possessing him.

Barb, trying to defuse the situation, said, "Do you have any idea what you're talking about? These are her *behaviors*. Is this your first nursing home?" Michael nodded. "You obviously have no idea what is normal for these people and what a typical morning looks like in a nursing home. Honey, I know you mean well, but you have to understand how a nursing home operates and how these people express their needs and 'work us' to get attention. If you hadn't had a visitor in almost two years, you'd yell out to strangers walking down the hall too, just for a little bit of human contact and attention." Barb took a quick breath and continued, "I know you meant well, but you don't know her clinical situation or how she exhibits behaviors and how we gauge when to go in there, and when we can, continue focusing on the other thirty-nine residents on this floor."

"I understand what you are saying, but—" Michael said.

Barb continued heatedly, her fist stabbing the air, and with a much more businesslike tone said, "If you would put one more nurse on the floor each shift and we had only thirteen or fourteen residents apiece and not twenty, maybe we could give them the kind of attention you're looking for. We aren't lacking compassion, trust me on that score. I've been doing this for seventeen years, thirteen here, and I am making almost half as much as my sister who's a nurse at the Brigham Hospital. Why? Well, because I love the elderly, and I care about the fact their minds are slipping from reality a little more each day. I don't like what the reimbursement system has done to the way we deliver care. It sucks that you—not you personally, but the powers that be—don't make the money anymore from Medicare, so with Medicaid as your only major source of income, you're stuck with more expenses than revenue. So what happens? You know already. The patients get fewer nursing hours, fewer CNA hours, poor laundry service, fewer activities, and the cheapest food your budget allows. Nice life, nice last stop for most of these people. I hope it doesn't happen to me, and you damn sure are thinking you hope this isn't your fate, huh?"

"Are you finished?" Michael asked. "I imagine not, and I am certainly not finished listening, but I have to get downstairs for the nine o'clock meeting. But you need to know I intend to rectify this and get this home back on the right track. First I need more time listening to your thoughts on what's wrong here."

"I'll stay late any night this week if you really mean it."

Michael knew she was right, but he also knew that however the residents got here and whatever the reimbursement system was and however it worked, he was determined they deserved the care their families could no longer—or chose to no longer—sustain for them. Every time he looked at Joan, Olivia, Bertha, or Lucy, he saw his grandmother, Alice. That was it. He was on fire and was going to set Paul, Barb, Peggy, Flo, and everyone else on fire to look at these people as more than just "residents." He made an appointment with the facility's administrator, Paul Thompson, for later that day. He was determined to get Paul on his team.

Our motto: In every interaction with one of our cherished residents, please think of him/her as if she were your grandmother or he were your grandfather. Thank you, Paul Thompson, Administrator

This sign appeared in the lunchroom by shift change that afternoon. It clearly caught a few sets of eyes. Some commented, some laughed, and one dietary aide actually cried. This might just be a new day. There were a few folks, though, who were less than passionate about Michael's fire that created this vision for the residents' lives.

"Oh for Christ's sake, he's a fucking cornball!" said Marylou, a salty old dog of a nurse, when she saw the sign.

Chapter 4: A Final Home

Verna

Peggy Godfrey, the admissions nurse, and Michael were driving through some of the tougher streets of Boston one Friday afternoon. They were trying to find the current home of Verna Bowen somewhere near the Codman Square section of Dorchester. Her daughter had called the day before asking in quick succession whether St. Matthew's had availability, accepted Medicaid, and could send someone to look at her mother.

The gang of hoods wasn't overly pleased to see these two professionally dressed white folks park their Volvo in front of a house that hadn't seen a paint job in about thirty years. In an attempt to look a little less white-bread yuppie, they shared a quick cigarette outside near the corner where they parked.

The house was a wreck. It was totally filthy and broken-down, smelling of urine, cigarettes, and stale alcohol. The daughter met them at the door. It was a single floor flat with barely a path to get from one room to the next. They were led into the kitchen where they found their future resident sitting on a daybed wedged between the stove and the refrigerator.

"This is my mother, Verna Bowen, who I called you about. She just can't stay here anymore. I need to get a job and she just can't be alone, can you, Ma? She's got that oldtimer's disease."

Speechless no longer, Michael started with, "The disease is actually called Alzheimer's and yes, older people are more prone to being diagnosed with it. But, more importantly, I think since Mrs. Bowen is sitting among us, it may be better to include her in the conversation and not exclude her from our discussion about her upcoming move—nor should we say anything that may upset her."

"You white folks always know the best way to treat and talk to our people, don't you? *She* doesn't know what we're talking about. That's why I called you. She needs to be in a nursing home. Your nursing home."

At this point Michael and Peggy both knew they had to accept her, regardless of her Medicaid status. They could not and would not keep her in this situation. If they didn't have a bed available, they would surely be calling protective services.

"I'd like to ask your mother a few questions," Michael said.

"Go ahead, just make it quick. And, what about today?"

Peggy, quiet until this point, chimed in, "What *about* today?"

"Can you get her out of here today? I just can't do it. She doesn't listen to me anymore and I need her bedroom for my son. His girlfriend kicked him out and he's been in trouble with the police lately, so I had to take him into custody here. Ma wets the bed too. Isn't that enough for you?"

Peggy said, "She actually needs a combination of three skilled needs and activities of daily living needs in order to be clinically eligible for Medicaid reimbursement. I am assuming your mother has Medicaid."

"Oh yeah, she does. They pay for all her doctor's bills and shit."

Michael had had enough. "Peggy, I am sure the clinical eligibility form won't be an issue. Let's just look at Mrs. Bowen's Medicaid card and talk about a move-in date." To her daughter, he said, "What does your mother want? What does Verna want? Ma'am, you need to take this into account. I know you have a lot on your plate, but is this really what is in her best interest? We are willing to take her to our nursing home, but—"

Michael was cut short by Verna's daughter. "I'm not interested in her interests right now. I am interested in my own, my interest in my sanity and my interest in my son. If I am going to keep my son off the crank, I need him to live here with me and that means she's got to go. Now, I know Medicaid pays for this and I know she doesn't know what she's talking about anymore. I also know she wets herself and even shits herself sometimes. So, if that isn't when and why the old ones go to a nursing home, then I don't know when they would."

"I understand this is a difficult time for you," Michael replied, "and I certainly am not saying St. Matthew's isn't a good place to take care of those who are unable to take care of themselves anymore. With all due respect, you need to understand that the minute an elderly or disabled individual can no longer take care of themselves, a nursing facility does not have to be the first or only option. It's just such a critical decision for you and your mother to make, I hope you are taking the time to work through it and make a decision you can live with."

Peggy couldn't hold back another second. "All right, I think you've heard enough of a lecture for one day. I need to take all the information and run it through the Medicaid regulations to ensure that Mrs. Bowen meets their eligibility in order for them to pay. We can figure this out for you. I'm pretty sure we can accommodate your mother and her needs. I *am* sorry, but we really didn't mean to lecture you. Michael just likes to educate every person and their family whom we consider for admission."

"Educate me on what?" asked her daughter, still not getting it.

"On the gravity of the situation and the decision to admit our loved ones to a long-term care facility—a nursing home," Michael said. "It truly is difficult for the person being placed and sometimes even more for the family managing the placement. And, we know there is often guilt associated with the decision. This often turns to a raw painfulness, the kind that will gnaw at you while you sleep, when you're praying, or when you're doing the dishes. We aren't saying that you are taking this lightly, it's just that you seem to be in a bit of a hurry. And thirty years from now, when you're elderly and your mother has been deceased for a while, and you try to remember her last months and years, your only memory will be of her six square feet of living space shared with another old lady, the permeating odor of urine and feces, and countless frustrating arguments and discussions with our staff regarding her care. This is inevitable because no care we provide can equal what you can give her here in her own home." He practically choked on this last statement.

Verna's daughter interrupted, "That part just isn't true. I know she'll have a roommate and that there will be odors. For Christ's sake, I deal with that now. But, you *can* provide the care I cannot. I don't know how to give her medications or to figure out what's wrong with her when she has a fever, or looks like she's going to fall, or has problems with her privates. Only nurses and nursing homes can do all that. I know you want to help me, but the only way you can help me is to take her. I got to take care of my son now. Her time has come and gone, and I got bigger fish to fry. He's got his whole life in front of him and she's done. I mean to say, her prime is done. Don't take that the wrong way."

"Oh, no, we wouldn't take *that* the wrong way," was all Peggy could muster.

The following Monday morning Verna arrived, walking through the front door with a sad-looking little brown plaid suitcase. Her daughter, two steps behind, seemed to only halfheartedly try to suppress a smile. It was clearly a smile of relief. She won her argument that her mother needed to be admitted for basic custodial nursing care. She was free of one generation and had a bedroom to give to the next generation. She knew she would get to the nursing home once a day. Well, that would be a good idea after she got organized; a good start would be every other day. After just a few days of catching up, she knew she'd easily slip into the every-other-day visits, or perhaps every third day.

Peggy was called to the foyer to greet Verna and fill out the paperwork. Her daughter asked Peggy just how long all this would take. Peggy responded, "Only about thirty to forty minutes. I just need you to sign the admissions agreement and learn alongside your mother all about her new home and Medicaid reimbursement rules."

"Just show me where to sign. I'm sure this won't take that long." Eyeing the inch-thick packet, she said, "I can read this the next time I'm here."

Having been through this routine before, Peggy knew not to push it. She assured the daughter she and the rest of the nursing team would take good care of Verna and call whenever there were issues or changes in Verna's condition. She added that the quarterly care plan meeting was very important and she should plan to attend to provide input when discussing Verna and her health status.

As Verna's daughter rushed out the door, she promised to attend one of these meetings as long as she got plenty of notice. As she walked to the sidewalk and began to take a left toward the waiting taxi, she ever so quickly turned her head to the side. Was it a look at the building or a chance to see her mother in the window of her new room? Or, as it turned out, was it a simple good-bye to the woman who brought her into this world fifty years ago? Regardless, no tear was shed. Peggy misted. Michael got a glimpse and ran to the men's room to cry in private and shield himself from judgment.

At 12:30 a.m. on Verna's first night at St. Matthew's, someone at the nurses' station heard a loud bang from down the hall. When the nurse, Maureen Cadogan, found her slumped on the floor next to her bed, Verna's head was soaked with blood from a relatively small gash. Maureen cleaned and bandaged the wound and helped her back to bed.

"Thank you, nurse. Where can I wait until my daughter comes to get me?"

"Oh, Verna, you need some rest. You've had quite a fall. I think you ought to lie down for a while." Maureen continued, "My name is Maureen and I'll be your nurse all night."

"Thank you, dear, but I won't need a nurse all night."

"Of course, Verna, but just in case your cut continues to bleed or causes you a headache, I'll be here. Let me help you into this bed so you can rest a bit." Slowly, then finally, there was no more resistance.

At 2:15 a.m., there was a scream from room 416. Josie was woken by her new roommate, Verna, shaking her bed and asking, "Who are you and why are you here?"

Josie yelled back, "I live here! This is my room. I'm Josie and you were put in my room earlier today. Now, go back to bed, you crazy old fool!"

"Help, help, get me out of here, I want to go home!" Verna cried repeatedly until Maureen came back.

"What's wrong here? Oh, honey, let me see your bandage. Come, sit on the bed with me." After a few minutes, Maureen convinced her to lie back down. There were numerous interjections inquiring about home, and how she was going there and not staying in a hospital.

At 5:40 a.m. Verna started again, "Get out of here! What are you doing in my house, you cracker lady?" The sun was starting to rise and Verna's nightmare wasn't ending anytime soon. Not to mention Josie's nightmare.

"I live here," Josie said. "This is a nursing home. My son and daughter-in-law put me here last year. I wet the bed a couple of times and that was it—they *just* couldn't do it anymore. I know you're a little confused. I was the first few nights, but you have to know that this is it. There is no turning back. Don't look back and don't beg to go back. They have already turned your room into something else—"

"I didn't have a room," Verna interrupted. "I lived off the kitchen."

"I'm sorry to hear that, dear. I'm Josephine. The nurses call me Josie. And, just so you know, I'm not loopy. I don't have that German disease—yet. And another thing, I don't care that you're black and I wouldn't dream of calling you one of those nasty names, so don't even think of calling me 'cracker' again."

"You got to help me, Josie. I don't belong here. I want to live with my daughter again. I was happy there. I didn't wet no bed and wasn't an imposition to no one. Who can I talk to about getting me out of here? You must know, you seem to know your way around."

"It's not that easy. No one leaves once they get here, unless they broke their hip and weren't meant to come here for long-term care. I think our children agree to that in the paperwork. There's some type of clause that says you won't take your old folks back, that you promise that this place gets to keep us forever."

"What did you say your name was again?"

"Josephine. Josie, from right here in Dorchester."

"Josie, you're crazy as a bedbug."

Chapter 5: George

Every nursing home has a ritual as frequent as daily or as infrequent as twice a week, but no home is complete without this high-frequency, high-stress activity called bingo. The gangs pack into the activity room, arriving an hour early to get a good seat, closest to the caller. Those who cannot hear get the front row, and those who cannot see get the rear seats because staff usually sit with them to put the red plastic discs on the numbers on the card. Emotions run pretty high.

George stood up abruptly, barely grabbing his walker as he shuffled awkwardly out of the activity room. The light yellow, slightly odorous trail ran down his leg and left a narrow, shallow puddle behind him. Too late. Oh, the embarrassment of it all. *Please, God*, George thought, *don't let anyone see it*. George headed as quickly as he could toward the downstairs men's room. Marie St. Jean, a CNA, sprinted after him.

"George, let's go upstairs and change your pants." This announcement didn't escape anyone sitting in various offices off this first floor hallway. "Why didn't you say something sooner? We could have gotten you to the bathroom sooner. You're wearing your diapers, aren't you?" She was good intentioned, but clueless when it came to terminology.

"Just let me get into the men's room alone," George begged.

"No, honey, we got to change your diapers."

"Please say 'underwear.' Would you want me saying that about you?" He had a strange, almost angry look on his face, like he might actually still be a human being with feelings.

By the time they got to George's room, Marie was grabbing onto his arm, gliding him along. "Oh, George, it *is* what it is. No one is listening and no one cares. It's just what happens to you guys when you get this old. There is nothing wrong with wearing diapers. It just helps you not to pee on the floor or in bed." She laid him on the bed, pulled his pants down, ripped the adhesive off the Depends, saw additional excrement, commented on *that*, wiped this away unceremoniously, and re-dressed him. "Good as new. Now, let's get you back downstairs."

"NO! I don't want to leave. I don't want to see anyone. Just leave me be." It didn't start as yelling, just firm and clear; clearly determined, anyway.

"It's only two o'clock, George. You can't just sit here until dinner at five. Don't you want to see all your friends downstairs? Bingo goes until three."

"No!"

"All right. See you later, George."

There he sat, facing the window, back to the door, slouched over, exhausted, embarrassed, and worn out. It rolled down, one long, salty stream. Then, suddenly, he couldn't turn them off. George sobbed quietly and then loudly to no one, for no one. Perhaps he was crying for his former self, his lost self? He turned slowly, peered into the mirror, and asked the stranger who he was and when this happened.

Wedged next to the window was the pressboard dresser with the broken drawers that didn't close all the way. The three on the left were for the other guy in the room and the three on the right were for George. Wedged between the wall and the window was a little nightstand. Adjacent to and hidden behind the door was the closet where George and his roommate each had a few articles of clothing hanging sloppily. The floor, a cheap schoolroom tile, was barely swept and had permanent skid marks from wheelchairs and walkers. *Is this really all that's left, all that I own? Is it really just what fits in half a room?* George was especially concerned with where his things went. He couldn't exactly put a finger on what the things were, but he knew he had things—was it furniture, clothes, a car? Regardless, they were gone.

Then, he had a flashback to a house and a woman in a tattered apron standing on the porch, looking down at the new 1959 Buick he was polishing. A house, a car, even a wife, perhaps? Where is that house now? Is she still alive, does she have the Buick? Were there dogs or were there children? And if so, where are *they* now? He looked in the mirror again and cried more tears. He wasn't presenting too well today, was he?

A few minutes later, George collapsed on his bed; when he woke, it was all forgotten. All he knew was that he was missing something, maybe it was bingo. George grabbed his walker, shuffled past the broken, partially-open drawers, and headed for the elevators without looking back.

Chapter 6: I Want to Go Home

Cherry

"I want to go home, please get me home! You do know that I still have a house. I have to get there to take care of it. You have to get me out of here." This was Cherry's daily, well, *hourly*, mantra. It was actually a mantra for many of the residents of this nursing home, especially those whose dementia had reached the point of no return. Sally had already seen it with Connie and George. It was that middle of the road where you have left earth just enough to know you are hanging in the balance between two worlds. The problem was that you wanted to be back on earth, but something told your mind you were really heading away from earth and its realities. In Cherry's case, earth was represented by her house or some semblance of a memory of that house.

One Tuesday afternoon in April—which could have been October as far as Cherry was aware—she roamed the halls, looking for what she had lost, and Cherry bumped into Doris. Doris was unknowingly checking out the faded wallpaper and the urine-stained floor. Actually, Doris wasn't really too sure what she was checking out, but while her mind raced between 1954 and 2008, she checked out the wallpaper from the vantage point of her wheelchair. This was all Cherry needed for an entrée.

"Hey, sweets, did you hang that wallpaper?"

"Hmmm?" Doris asked.

"It looks like you know it intimately, and it's old enough to be something you could have been capable of, right, dear?"

"It's pretty. Those are cornflowers. I grew them in my garden."

"You did, huh? A garden of wallpaper. At least you know you lived somewhere else. Half these old coots don't know where they are and where they're from and, for that matter, where they're going. Where did you live, honey? And do you think you're going back?"

"Oh, I have a husband and a daughter, but I don't know where they live today. I lived there with them, back in the day. We all did, we all lived with our families. Maybe they're coming today. I saw them last day, no, last year."

"What does that mean, 'last day' or 'last year'?" Cherry asked a very confused Doris.

"I know. I saw the nurse. See her over there. She wants my blood pressure." Doris had a way of looking at Cherry during some of her rambling answer, but more often than not she stared at the wallpaper or toward the ceiling as she provided answers to her new friend. Her dementia was mid-stage, allowing her the benefit of an occasional glimpse into reality, into today. Inversely, her disease allowed Cherry to glimpse backward to her youthful days. Then came the blur. Did the memory keep her in that era or did the memory fade and bring Doris back to today and the stench of urine on the floor? Cherry certainly didn't know the answer. She was just looking for a co-conspirator in her quest to get out of there and find her home.

Cherry continued unabashedly, "So, are you going back or not?"

"Going back where?"

"Oh, Jesus Christ, you're kidding me! Isn't anyone sane around here?"

The tone, the word "sane," and the dizzying circular conversation took Doris so far away into the wallpaper scanning project that Cherry gave up.

"Missy, you there!" Cherry was off to the nurses' station to participate in some conversation that might resemble normalcy. "Can you help me get home?"

"Ma'am, this is your new home," MaryLou told Cherry. "You've come to stay with us. You need to be here because you require around-the-clock nursing. People like me will give you your medicine throughout the day, and we'll make sure you don't fall and that you don't wander off."

Cherry laid into her. "First off, don't 'Ma'am' me. I have a name and it is Cherry Jordan. You can call me Miz Jordan or Cherry. Second, I ain't no child, so don't be talking about wandering off like a kid at the county fair would. Next, I know how and when to take my medication. In summary, Lady Jane, that's why I'm getting out of here as soon as my son gets called. You're allowed one phone call, right? I need to talk to my son."

MaryLou couldn't help herself and the paradigm she'd been operating in as she continued to patronize Cherry.

"Yes, that's right, you have a son. The records show that Mr. Henry Jordan lives in Milton. Is that right? Your son must be your guardian, so I will contact Michael in social services to ensure that he knows Henry's thoughts and wishes, and then we'll take it from there."

Cherry was fuming and understood enough to realize that something was off and she was in some sort of rabbit hole that was getting curvier and deeper by the minute. "What does this mean, this word 'guardian'? Who is Michael, and why can't I keep having a conversation with this woman in front of me who seems to be in charge, or perhaps a nurse? Why? And what is this other place and person? Why couldn't that lady staring at the wallpaper help me, and why does this place have to smell so badly of piss? Don't they take baths here, for cryin' out loud?"

So, she asked instead, "I'm my own person. I *am* the boss of my son. He is not the boss of me, and I don't rightly even know what this guardian talk is all about and what they do. Let's keep this real simple. These people are pissin' and shittin' themselves and I am not getting out. No, getting in, staying in, that is. So, help me stay out of here."

Throughout her diatribe, Cherry was unaware of the fact her arms were flailing and pointing and that the nurse was trying to calm her down by gently taking hold of her left wrist. It happened all at once. Cherry's arm hit the nurse's face. The nurse screamed out about a code "something"— black, white, or blue—which was announced on a loudspeaker.

Susan Sullivan was first on the scene. "Grab her, hold her down, she's dangerous! Her record mentions anxiety disorder so there's got to be an order for Haldol or something. If there is, prepare a shot for an IM Haldol injection. Hurry, stat!"

Susan ran behind the nurses' station, made a call to a nurse practitioner and Cherry's doctor's office, scribbled a note in the record authorizing it, and loaded the solution into a needle. At this point Jon Ramos, a CNA, had arrived on the scene.

Susan yelled, "Jon, grab her! This one right here," and pointed to Cherry. Jon, not one to miss a workout at the gym, grabbed Cherry's arm with his left hand and swung his right arm around her middle.

"I've got her."

While Jon held tight, Susan took the needle and jammed it into Cherry's arm. When it found its way through her flesh, Susan pulled on the syringe to release the Haldol into Cherry's bloodstream. Intramuscular—no faster way to achieve the desired effect. A minute later, Cherry couldn't even stand. As her knees buckled, she started falling to the floor.

As Jon walked back to his unit, he turned to encourage his colleague. "It works every time. She'll shut up now." He added, "By the way, Susan, who was the doc who pulled through for us?"

"It was actually Kathy O'Neill, the doc's NP. She hates to bother him and knows how we need some peace around here, especially when the sun-downing starts." Susan knew it was against state public health regulations to sedate or drug one of their residents to simply stifle them and allow more quiet time for the staff. On some level, she always knew what was right from what was wrong. Susan knew that when the 11 p.m. to 7 a.m. nurses turned the volume down to zero on the call bell master console at the nurses' desk, they were creating a system that didn't give the residents a fighting chance to get the care they needed and deserved throughout the night. But, as righteous as she liked to believe she was, she always seemed to manage to let this slide.

The question was, what else slides around here?

Charlotte

Charlotte didn't know who she was anymore and what her name was, though she would respond to "Jane" sometimes, but no one knew why. She arrived at "The Center" about two years ago. Apparently she had two sons and two other daughters, but the staff saw only one daughter. This was fairly typical, but it did strike one CNA as particularly sad that, mathematically, she got only a twenty percent return on investments. Isn't that why people have children, to continue their legacy? Because it's God's plan to procreate, but more importantly to insure there's someone to take care of you when your cycle of life starts cycling south? So in the CNA's estimation, this poor old lady—and she sure was poor—gave her heart, soul, and effectively her life to birth and raise five children, but when it came to her turn for care, she was dumped into a nursing home. How could one of five not find it in their schedule or financial plan to stay home and take care of an elderly mother with increasing signs of dementia?

So now only one sibling got to this godforsaken place a few times each week. Charlotte's daughter, Julie, didn't see it at first, but then the subtle and not-so-subtle signs emerged. There were the word retrieval issues— "The, the, the little gadget thing that you put your jewelry in, you know what I mean!" Then, there was calling her daughter by the nurse's name or Charlotte's sister's name. Then, there was coming to visit and smelling the distinct odor of fecal matter emanating from her mother's slacks. Yes, indeed, Julie was slowly watching her mother's march toward a steep and narrow stairway to death. What was she going to do? Leave her job and bring her mother home and take a crash course in nursing? And figure out how to dispense medications, how to clean private areas, and how to deal with urinary tract infections and fainting spells? How does one suddenly make that move, that courageous yet possibly unsafe and life-changing move? Julie sure felt paralyzed when faced with such a dilemma. She had a certain recollection of her mother and her Aunt Melissa dealing with a similar dilemma when they placed their mother, Julie's grandmother, in a nursing home. Julie clearly recalled thinking that she would not—ever—do this when the time came for her own mother.

Julie found herself knocking on the door to social services on her way toward the front door. Sally and Michael were both scribbling away in medical charts, keeping up with their social services notes requirement. Sally asked if she could help with something.

"So," Julie asked Sally, "what happened to the promise I made to myself never to put my mother in a nursing home to see her rotting away here? How did I go so far from being so sure that I couldn't do this to my mother today, when I am sitting watching her stare off into space while she sits in her own feces. What kind of daughter am I anyway?"

As Julie left Sally's office, Sally thought, *Another story, another day. Julie isn't that different from so many other adult children of St. Matthew or Country Manor or Shady Side Estates. Or is she? Maybe Julie truly had no other choice, while Doris's daughter Jessica or Verna's daughter did seem to have choices. How would those choices have played themselves out?* Sally told Michael, "Welcome to another day in the lives of the demented ones who continue to live without will, choice, or understanding of where they are or who they've become." Michael just sighed a heavy sigh.

The ride home wasn't too pleasant. Julie's cell phone rang three times, her husband and two daughters all calling separately with questions and needs. Every pothole, red light, and rude driver yielded a "Fuck this!" Listening to the unanswered calls, now excitable voicemail messages, Julie was reminded how needed she was to solve an issue, fix a dinner, and do a soccer practice pick-up. Then, late at night, she found time for a PowerPoint presentation "clean up" job so her big-shot husband would look good in the office the next day.

So didn't Mom carry this weight for all of us forty years ago? Julie thought. *Yeah, Dad left over too many fights, money issues, and Mom yelling about his gambling. Yes, we had to help around the house so Mom could work five days a week to keep the household going. Yes, she sat with me and worked on my homework for an hour or so, then helped my learning-disabled brother for another couple of hours before she passed out from exhaustion.* Julie kept coming back to the same haunting question. *Why did I do this, then? What was my thought process that day I admitted her to this hellhole? Was it fear of her wandering or my fear that I wouldn't keep my family together if I attempted to be the one of the five, the only caring one, to take her in?*

Chapter 7: Transition
Night at St. Matthew

Frannie barely took her last breath. That was it, no fanfare or Hollywood movie ending for her. If this had been an ad about the dangers of smoking, Frannie's cigarettes were sitting on her nightstand, so a movie camera could have zoomed in on the Newport Lights, then they could add a dirty ashtray and suddenly transition to the dying woman with the sunken-in cheeks from too much heavy inhaling over the past fifty-five years. Frannie was only sixty-eight. Sixty-eight years old, living in a nursing home for three years and dying there only three years after her untimely admission.

No one was there to capture this moment, or to say goodbye, or to tell Frannie her life wasn't lived in vain. With no call bell ringing, no one knew another resident was in need of something; she wasn't in need of medications or a diaper change, but simply someone to stand by her bed and hold her hand while she passed from one world to the next. But Frannie experienced none of this when she went through her transition. It was a lonely death compared to that of many former residents of St. Matthew. But then again, what human being can really grasp what Frannie experienced and if *she* even felt that it was lonely? For all anyone knows, a human being's hand means nothing when a spirit is leaving its body and becoming one with the sun or the moon, or God, or whatever we become when we leave our body. But the nurses who have held the hands of the dying were always pretty sure it meant something to the lonely soul who was going through that final transition.

It was 6:45 a.m. the next morning. Marie St. Jean entered Frannie's room to wake her up. A chill went down her spine as the cold, hard reality of death greeted her like a scream in the dark. But she didn't jump back. Her grandmother once taught her that the dead can't hurt you, that it's the living who can do you harm. It must have sunk in as she methodically pulled the call bell cord to summon assistance. She walked to the other side of the room, woke the roommate, ceremoniously transferred her to her wheelchair, and wheeled her out to the hall, all without saying a word. Only then did Marie reenter the room, bless herself, and pull the sheet over Frannie's head. By then Flo had run in to see what had happened. Flo gasped, composed herself, then pulled the sheet down to ensure there was no pulse. She looked at her watch and, as if reading a cereal box, said, "Time of death: 6:30 a.m." This was just an estimation, but something was needed for the death certificate.

"Poor Frannie. She had a lousy life, then a lousy, lonely death. Her last days spent in this dumpy little room," Flo said.

"But Flo, we did everything to make her later years as nice as can be. We took her outside to smoke. We talked to her about her life and her past. What else was I supposed to do when she was one of twelve patients assigned to me on a shift?"

"I guess besides finding a way to get her out of here alive, there wasn't much else you could have done. You did care for her and Frannie knew it. She really knew it. We all tried for her. That's our lot in life here—to pick up the pieces and play surrogate daughters to these lonely souls whose children weren't up to the task. Anyway, I gotta go. I still have another half a floor that needs meds passed. Will you wait here until the funeral director arrives?"

Just another passing at St. Matthew's. Back to work. Housekeeping came into the room the minute the funeral directors left with the body. The bed was stripped, the pillows removed and tossed. The social worker came in with a large black garbage bag and methodically dumped all the contents of Frannie's two bureau drawers into the bag. This was the "belongings bag" that was thrown together to give to the next of kin.

How sad to think of a lifetime of accumulation of things, furniture, or perhaps real estate, but when all was said and done, this was it. After dying in a nursing home, it was a couple of garbage bags full of odds and ends. And so it goes.

"Where's Frannie?" asked Bertha and a few other residents who still possessed a degree of their faculties. "I haven't seen her going out for a cigarette yet. Isn't she feeling well?"

"Oh, Bertha, stop! She's gone. Plain and simple. Just like Nellie last week, Francine the week before, and Katherine the week before that. This isn't just a stop along the way, dear. This is the last stop on the train called life. Where's Frannie? We all know where she is and most of us saw it coming. But what's more important here, and let's just talk about it, is that we really don't care. Not in the way that we don't give a darn, but more that we know it's coming and frankly, we just aren't surprised anymore. It's what happens here, and the only reason it doesn't happen sooner from the day we're admitted here is because of the tons of meds they shove down our throats, which of course is in our best interest, right? They *are* doing the right thing to keep us alive because it's the humane thing to do or because the department of public health forces them to do everything they do to us. I mean for us." Rita was on a rampage.

"Oh, dear, what are you talking about? What is this talk about living and dying and staying alive through too many medications? I think you're being distasteful and disrespectful to poor Frannie, who has just died an unfortunate death."

"Unfortunate? What about the death of a penniless, frail eighty-four-year-old who had nothing to live for and died in her sleep do you find so unfortunate? I have to tell you it is what it is here and nothing more. We have no one to take care of us and no one who has the money to buy the home care services to keep us at home, so we're sent here. It's nothing more and nothing less. Look at Doris over there. Do you think that in her catatonic state it would be so unfortunate the day she dies here? Don't you think that beneath that shell of a façade, there is half a brain that is saying 'Uncle! I'm done and I've had enough pain and suffering for one life!' Or look at Charlotte. She sits day after day with that thinly painted half-smile not knowing who she is or who she was. That crazy sister of hers visits her every week, talking to her like Charlotte understands a single word she is saying. It does make me wonder why they don't give up. What do they need from us, our family members who come here out of a sense of obligation while we sit here and stare at them or drool for a little extra measure? Ha! They say the same stupid things and talk about the same mundane subjects from their life that really don't affect or impact us anymore, do they? You know what it is, don't you, Mary?

"It's plain and simple guilt. Guilt—the most underrated human emotion. They're feeling guilty that they dumped us here, or another family member dumped us here, and they did nothing but silently watch it happen."

At this point half the room was listening or half listening. Wheelchairs were propelling toward the center of this un-heard of conversation. Only those in the most demented states didn't bend an ear.

Joan piped up for the first time in almost a year. "You know what I don't understand? They wouldn't have to feel guilty if they had just listened to us in the first place! I mean, really, who here was an active participant in the discussion that led to your being left here like yesterday's garbage? I wish my son and daughter-in-law had asked me, 'Gee, Mom, how would you like to live in a nursing home? How would you like to leave behind, never to be seen again, all your belongings except for a few articles of clothing that can fit into two drawers of a broken-down bureau? And how would you like to leave the queen-size bed you have slept in for years to be supplanted with a tiny single bed that is about three feet away from a stranger you have never laid eyes on in your life?' Or, if only she would have said, 'Do you have any thoughts or issues with living on a ward with forty other old ladies and a few dirty old men, where your only private space is a so-called semi-private room where the door never closes and there's only a thin little curtain between you and your roommate? And did I remember to tell you I did some research and over the past year, five employees have been cited for allegedly abusing patients and only three patients have died from causes that required an autopsy?' No, she didn't. But if she had, I probably would still be sitting here bitching about the fact it happened."

Michael walked in during the heat of the conversation and worried that this wasn't the kind of healthy talk the residents should be engaging in. He always thought the nursing home residents needed to speak happy talk and not focus on the aspects of the nursing home that did not remind them of their former homes. Nor should they be focusing on how or why they came to be living there. He certainly didn't think they should be disparaging their families, who had made very difficult decisions when admitting their mother or father to this home.

"So," Michael began, "what is all this talk I'm hearing? Bertha, I'm surprised at you. I thought you would have helped cheer everyone up, possibly start a trivia game or even some bingo. You've all been so happy here. We're doing the best we can for you, aren't we? Please tell me if there is something more I can do for you."

Joan countered with, "No, you don't understand, we don't dislike the nursing home and we realize it's our permanent residence, so in effect, I guess it is our home. But it will never be the home we lived in, the four walls we gave up or were forced to leave so suddenly. Why couldn't we have had just one more year, or even one more day, before moving to this final stop?"

Michael continued, clearly without listening, "You were part of that decision. I spoke in detail with each and every one of your families when they came into my office seeking a new home for you that could meet your physical needs. They *did* talk to you about your transition to your new home."

No less than three began to reply all at once. "Talk to us, not at us!" "We're right here, and we're not idiots. We know who we are and what happened to us." "We like you and think you're doing good things here, but you don't 'get it' that we are making the best of it, but we wouldn't have *chosen* this. Let me ask you, would you have chosen this for *your* mother?"

"I love each one of you like you're my family, but I don't understand what you're saying," said Michael. "Of course I talk to you. What do you mean by talking 'at' you? Clearly, you must be confusing me with other staff. Are you saying some of the staff do not treat you respectfully? If so, that's a serious breach of conduct and not what we require at St. Matthew."

"No, we're not," Joan said clearly. "You mean well, but really, look around, and I ask you again, would you allow your own mother to live here? And if so, would she have come here perfectly willingly or kicking and screaming? Seriously, tell us now!"

Michael replied, "I am being serious and need you to understand you are wanted and loved here. Your families also love you and certainly loved you when you were living with them or in your own home." He spoke with only a slight bit of desperation in his voice. He was trying to convince either himself or the people who were speaking the truth.

They looked at him with eyes brimming with bewilderment and a hint of sarcasm.

Chapter 8: The Hamiltons

It was a cute little suburban home outside of Boston's Route 128 beltway, tucked into a cul-de-sac in a working class town called Canton. Joan's son, Luke, was heading out the back kitchen door to throw some steaks on the grill. Luke told his wife, Katie, that tonight he would *finally* clear out his mother's room and get a few garbage bags full of her old stuff ready for the Salvation Army. He had won the coin toss to turn the room into a "man cave." Katie would have to wait until one of their children went to college to get her sewing room. Katie expressed her thanks to God that the room was *finally* getting cleaned out and prepared. It had, after all, been three days since they moved Luke's mom, Joan Hamilton, to St. Matthew's.

"How are you doing, honey?" Katie asked Luke with a hint of sincerity. "I know we needed to do it, but she *is* your mother."

"You're right, dear; we had to do it. It was time, and we just couldn't do it anymore. She was confused and didn't even know where she was half the time. Remember last week when Ma called me my brother's name? Like I even look the least bit like Mark. Really? But it really hit me when we smelled the urine on the family room couch. It just wasn't fair to you, and I wasn't going to live, I mean, let you live like that. You have enough going on. But I do thank you for all your patience. It was a rough couple of years, especially the last few months."

"It sure was, honey, but at least it's over and we have that room back, and we won't have to be spraying Febreze anymore and worrying about stinky carpets and furniture."

"You're a good sport, Kate; that's why I love you!" Kate was rewarded for dumping her mother-in-law with a big wet kiss. "Let's eat!"

After dinner, Luke dug into his little project to turn his mother's former bedroom into his perfect hideaway—or was it getaway?— from his wife, son, and daughter. He had heard on television that this was called a "man cave" and was pumped up even further by this thought tonight.

"Honey, I want to go in the morning and take this notebook I found."

"What notebook, Luke?"

"This one I found when cleaning mom's room last night. She had been writing in it over the years. It's not so much a diary as a catalog of her life's events. I want to take it to the nursing home in the morning."

"Luke, don't do that. Whatever it is, she doesn't know she's missing it. I never saw her using it here. Also, she'll think you're there so soon because you're bringing her back here. Don't confuse her. She needs at least a week to go by without us haunting her with self-centered visits that are really all about, um, well . . ."

"All about what, Kate? What is it you're not finishing? Typical for you, isn't it?"

"I was almost there, actually. About making us feel better. There. We only go there because we feel guilty that we kicked her out of here."

"Fuck you, Kate! We did not kick her out of here. We were told by every friend and family member who has a clue about this kind of thing that we just couldn't do it anymore. No one wanted to lay a guilt trip on us, and they knew what we were going through. We aren't nurses or doctors, and we don't know if we are crushing her spine when we transfer her from her wheelchair to her bed. I don't feel guilty, because I did what I had to do."

"That's it, simply what *you had* to do. I don't recall you looking at home health care or respite type options."

"That's funny, Kate, because I don't recall you doing that either. You love to pontificate, but you're a little lacking in the lead-by-example category, you bitch!"

"She's NOT my fucking mother! It's not my place to lead by example, and by the way, if you ever call me by that word again, you will be very sorry. Oh, and by the way, *you* are a fucking prick."

"OK, all-righty then. Let's take a deep breath." After sinking in his chair and grabbing the glass of wine that had been inviting him all night, he finally mustered some courage.

"Kate, I really don't care about your motives for doing anything. As far as my taking my mother her notebook, it *is* all about her and has nothing to do with me. I am looking to help her and not confuse her. Clearly, I'll be careful to explain she can't come home. I'll focus on the need for the round-the-clock nursing care we just couldn't provide or afford. This hasn't been easy on me either, you know, so I am not going to make it worse by upsetting her."

"Take her the fucking notebook," Kate replied with complete and utter resignation.

The next morning Luke parked outside St. Matthew Nursing Home. As he got out of his Ford Taurus, his lungs created quite a stir with some major coughing, culminating in a bit of spit up. Tears streaming down his face, Luke turned around toward the car. He stopped, stared, and felt nothing but silence and a cold, hollow feeling. After a few minutes and catching his breath, Luke mustered the courage to walk toward the entrance to his mother's new home. It is her home, isn't it? Luke continued to ponder where her life was now and what his role was in her life-changing event. Luke wanted to believe it was all Kate's fault, but when you get to be alone with your thoughts you have some time for honesty with yourself.

Walking in the front door, there were no open arms to greet him. The admissions director must surely work only Monday through Friday because she wasn't here on this Sunday morning. She wasn't here to ask him if he had had second thoughts. No, she wouldn't do *that* anyway. Her job was to keep the place full, not offer assistance to a guilty son who thought he'd made a mistake. Neither Sally nor Michael from the social services department was anywhere to be found. Luke was also informed there was no administrator or director of nursing here today. He had some questions he was hoping to get answered about his mom's care, and there were some other general rules and policies he needed clarified. Luke was eventually steered toward Flo, the crusty old third floor nurse who was "acting supervisor" today.

"Mrs. Hamilton did OK last night, Mr. Hamilton," Flo reported.

"What does 'OK' mean? I find it hard to believe she was fine throughout her first night staying here after living in my home for the past two years."

"Are you saying you'd rather your mother *didn't* have a pleasant first night here? Would that be such a terrible thing? I know a nursing home can have a bad rap sometimes, but we're here all day and all night doing everything possible for these people. We hold their hands at night when they're crying." Flo forgot to mention all the times she and her colleagues were at the nurses' station listening to music, chewing the fat, and filling out the reams of required paperwork. "We run down the hall when they ring their call bells for our attention. We literally don't stop from the moment we get in until we leave at the start of the next shift."

"Ah, um, I really didn't mean to imply anything to do with your work habits or how diligently you perform your duties. And I hope you understand I do want my mother to have a comfortable night. I am trying to reconcile how she could be in a brand new place after all those years in familiar territory in her own bedroom in my wife's and my home."

In the most deadpan manner, Flo retorted, "Did you ever think she wanted to get out of that familiar little territory under your roof?"

"Wait a minute, no . . ."

Flo continued, "Could it be possible that this place, in her mind, might give her a little bit of independence?"

"All right, miss, I've had just about enough. I have struggled with the decision for months now. One doesn't take putting their mother into a nursing home lightly, and then you're telling me she might have wanted this?"

"I am just telling you that you don't have to feel so guilty about sending her here. You're convinced because of societal views that you 'dumped' her. There seems to be a baseline assumption that this is a dump, that even to consider placing an elderly relative into a nursing home is evil and means you are a terrible son. I haven't given my entire adult life to this profession because I think it's a dump or because I enjoy hanging around a dump for fifty-plus hours a week. Are you really feeling guilty because you don't have the stomach to clean your mother's bottom after she's moved her bowels? Is that the crime you think you've committed? I'm certainly not implying that a son or daughter shouldn't do that as much as humanly possible, but isn't there a tipping point where it's just not possible anymore? Should she sit in her shit for hours until one of you comes home from work? Or who's going to make sure she doesn't light the stove and then drop paper towels onto the gas flame? What about after she falls trying to walk down the stairs from one room to the next and—"

"All right, I get it. I guess you already know my mother well. I am not saying it's a poor choice to send your mother to a nursing home, and I am not saying this is a bad one. If it was, I wouldn't have chosen it. I did tour three and this one was the cleanest and had the least odor of urine. My point is that I have known neighbors who hired a caretaker during the day. It's costly, but at least you can keep working and you don't have to see your mother, um, well, you know . . ."

"Mr. Hamilton, you're looking for the word 'institutionalized.' That's what the critics call it."

"Luke, please. Please call me Luke. And you're Flo, right?" Flo nodded. "Yes, I am embarrassed and ashamed of myself that my own mother lives in an institution. That I, well, that I institutionalized her. And, one of the reasons was to keep the peace between my wife and me."

"Oh, the big, bad daughter-in-law routine. She pushed for this—to get old mama out of the way—and now you're feeling guilty that the second woman in your life had the power to put away the first woman, and you basically sat back and allowed it or even facilitated it?"

Luke looked absolutely shocked. "What are you, clairvoyant or something? How do you know these things? And why are you trying to help me?"

"Honey, I'm an old black lady who has been around a long time. I've seen it all. But more importantly, I'm going to be stuck with you. You obviously care as you're here on day two. So, I think you're going to be in my hair a lot over the next few years. The less guilt you feel, the easier my job is going to be."

"I'm sorry, I don't get the connection?"

"Mr. Hamilton, I mean Luke, I have some pills to push and bottoms to wipe. I'll talk to you again. Just ask for Flo, unit three, B wing, first shift."

Chapter 9: Resident Council

Tuesdays at eleven in the morning. There was no better time of the week, except for the bingo games held on Mondays and Fridays at two in the afternoon. Bertha was the first to arrive, followed by Joan and Olivia. Some were escorted by a CNA pushing their wheelchair, while others were able to self-propel. Perhaps it was just an opportunity to get out of their rooms, but for those who hadn't been overtaken with dementia, it was an opportunity to speak your mind and still have an opinion. Plus, the coffee and Danish were nothing to sneeze at.

Carol Jansen, the activities director, ushered everyone in starting at 10:30. Soon there were twenty-three people sitting around the table with Styrofoam cups filled with lukewarm coffee at each place. Millie Harris, the president of the Resident Council, asked Carol if it was all right to start the meeting. Carol told her it was just about eleven and to wait a few minutes longer.

"Why can't we start now?"

"John is always late. He'll get here when he gets here. Can't we just start?"

"Yeah, I've got things to talk about that can't wait."

"Oh, really? What can't wait? What topics are going to rush out the door while we sit here for a few minutes? And what is so important that will change anything about our lives here?"

This chatter continued for about ten minutes until Carol had to try and break it up before someone's feelings got hurt.

"Everything we discuss is important and affects our lives here at St. Matthew's. We'll all have a chance to talk about what's on our mind once a couple more of our regulars get here."

When John and Verna both strolled in with their CNA's help, Carol nudged Millie to start.

As the Resident Council president, one of Millie's official duties was to call the meeting to order. As activities director, Carol then guided Millie through the standard agenda items, which polled the residents gathered on how they were feeling about services lately—nursing, activities, dining, laundry, housekeeping, and rehab services as applicable.

Millie bellowed, "Let's start this meeting! Who's got something to say?"

"What do you want us to say?" asked John. "Yeah, I could tell you lots of things but don't know what people want to hear."

All hell proceeded to break loose starting with Frannie. "We don't want to hear anything you have to say."

"Millie does all the talking all the time. Can't we hear more from Joan or Mary? They never say a word."

"If that crazy Bertha starts one more time with her 'Life is beautiful' crap, I'm going to throw up all over this table. It's like she's living in that stupid eighties movie *Cocoon*."

Then Verna asked, "Who are you people and why do you live in my home? And what happened to that lady who was sleeping in another bed in my bedroom?"

Carol watched blankly as if her voice were paralyzed. She kept thinking she should say something, but considering these meetings usually focused on how many times a week bingo was offered or whether it could be offered an additional day, she was rather enjoying the study presenting itself. What happened next stunned her into a continued silence.

Olivia started, "Josie died. Two days ago. Didn't anyone tell you? Rather, I ask, why didn't anyone tell you? We are sent here to die, aren't we? You once said that to me, George. I know you did. It's the normal cycle of life—the beginning, the early middle, the middle, early end, and the almost end. You wouldn't be sent here if it wasn't the almost end. This IS where we are sent to die. Once we slow down, and we are not *useful* to our families anymore, are in the way, and of course, when we first start wetting our pants, then our bags get packed."

Mary said, "I want to go home, now. I can learn to be useful again. It's my home, isn't it? I'm not dead yet, and I could live a few more years."

"But what about that woman who was in my room?" Verna asked.

Olivia tried again. "Her name was Josephine Cruz, and she lived here for five years. Her only child, a son, and his wife were better than most and came here almost every day. She had a life before they sent her—*had to* send her—to

St. Matthew's. Josephine once told me she was from Puerto Rico and came to America when she was twenty, some seventy years ago. She lost a daughter to tuberculosis when she was still a young mother, not quite thirty. Josie worked up the street on Washington in her husband's grocery store, six days a week for almost sixty years. He dies. The son sells the bodega and tells ma to move in with him as she won't have enough to do without the store, and she can help around his house and with his two young sons. Who says no to their only child? Husband, home, and job, all gone within a matter of months. What do you think happened to her?" Silence. "Oh, come on, you all know the answer. Short answer: we end up here. Even shorter answer: we die here. But we all know what happens—we start giving up. When our mind isn't busy thinking, working, planning, helping, it slows down, and this goes hand in hand with our bodies. Yes, I think losing control of our bladder and bowels is related to having less to do and feeling as if we are becoming a nobody within our family realm."

"But why does that give them the right to send us here? From what you just said, it isn't our fault. Didn't they help cause our falling down, so to speak? Didn't our collective sons and daughters make the decisions to slow us down, sometimes under the guise of protecting us?"

George asked what the hell "guise" meant.

Bertha implored the team to reconsider such serious discussions and harsh indictments of each other's sons and daughters. "I don't have any children," she said, "but if I did, I wouldn't talk about them this way, and furthermore, if I did have one, she would never do something like that. I'd still be living with her. I am only here because I was alone in the world. I had the accident and needed some rehab. Didn't you all have some type of hospitalization due to an illness, accident, or a serious incident like a stroke? I don't think it was all a matter of someone's daughter saying, 'I don't need you here anymore.' Now really, let's be civil."

"Verna's did. I saw it. I was sitting in my wheelchair. She barely handed her own mother off to Nurse Peggy, and she spun around on her heels and was out the door. I swear to God to this very day that I never saw that woman look back."

"Olivia, don't say that 'bout my daughter. She is just doing some remodeling of her home and taking care of her sick son. This is temporary," Verna chimed in.

"Oh, honey, you're right. I am sure you'll be home before you know it." Bertha reassured Verna as best she could even though it wasn't clear to too many if she believed her own words anymore. There had been too many lies about the reality that was and is St. Matthew's. It was just typically from the mouths of the staff.

George brought things back a bit. "Josie's dead? When the hell did this happen? They think we're all a bunch of demented imbeciles. I don't understand why they think we aren't part of the process here. You know, we live here, like it or not. If one of us kicks the bucket, shouldn't we all grieve, sort of like a family would? That's what my family did when my wife died. Everyone was informed—kids, grandkids, her sisters, my cousins, our neighbors. How could we all grieve together for Lily if people weren't even informed? Even Verna didn't know enough to mention today that Josie is dead."

"I liked Josie, sweet little lady before the dementia or whatever it's called that happens to our brains got to her. I also heard her great stories about the old country, the grocery store, her wonderful husband Raul. Carol, I want to have a wake for Josie. Can you make that happen?" George asked.

Carol had heard a lot of this talk and a saw lot of blank stares, a lot of arguing and raised voices, but it was never clear who was saying what and if they knew what they were saying. When Carol or Peggy or Flo or Lea saw the blank stares, they sometimes filled in the blanks with what could have been a voice in the dialogue. But there was no mistaking when George asked her if there could be a wake for Josephine Cruz, who died six days ago and was already somewhere six feet under at the nearby Cedar Grove Cemetery.

"Oh, George, how sweet of you to think about Josie Cruz. She was a dear and used to attend these very same Resident Council meetings. She always had nice suggestions about activities we could do, especially getting outside in the nice weather. Do you remember when we did the indoor gardening last January at her suggestion? We grew tomato vines in eggshells. How lovely."

All the while, George was staring at her with an increasingly twisted face. "Carol, I meant an 'after-funeral wake' like they do over in the United Kingdom. I haven't lost my mind like some of my friends here. I know she's dead, and I want to make sure the others know too. I think we need to, you know, talk about it."

"George, do you think we ignore death here or sweep it under the carpet?"

"Well, Carol, we certainly do a good job pretending it doesn't exist. I know many of us don't have our wits about us, but plenty like me, at least, have some wits. We know there isn't another stop after this. This is the last stop, isn't it?"

Bertha walked out of the room, walker in hands, and softly spoke to the group over her shoulder. "All I know is that I am happy it is the last stop. I was pretty lonely living in my apartment alone."

A lot of people would not agree with Bertha, and many at the table had no idea what she was saying or what it meant. Others frowned in vehement disagreement. Carol was heartened to hear that she and her colleagues must really be doing a good job, that someone actually wanted to be here and thought it was a better alternative to living in a lonely apartment with no one to talk to. Many sons and daughters, nieces and nephews would have felt a hundred-pound weight slowly melting from their guilt-laden shoulders. The more cynical or deeply-rooted guilty ones would have thought Bertha was just nuts, and that was why she actually liked living in a nursing home among the constant smell of piss, crap, and death in the air, despite not having the physical frailties to qualify to live there.

Nevertheless, she said it and her words hung in the air like smoke from a campfire.

Chapter 10: Dinnertime

St. Matthew's, as well as all nursing homes in the country, is required by regulation to offer lunch and dinner in a communal setting, typically in the form of a large, impersonal dining room. St. Matthew's adorned the dining room walls with crucifixes and portraits of the Blessed Virgin Mary, just a little something to personalize the room. The tables were dressed with oilcloth tablecloths, paper napkins, metal place card holders that contained a listing of each resident's food allergies, type of diet—as in whole food, ground food, or mush—and a listing of food likes and dislikes.

Sally had been rounding the facility more often and started observing the routines and schedules, and realized just how routinized these people's lives had become. Starting at 4:30, those who self-propelled their chairs, or who could walk with or without a walker or cane, began arriving for the highlight of the day. Depending on whether the afternoon activity was good, interesting, or attractive to a resident and lasted beyond 2:30, this was their first chance to do something before nightfall and another night of interrupted sleep and listening to their roommate snore.

The aides started getting the residents in wheelchairs down by the elevator doors by 4:45 in the afternoon. When the institutional looking kitchen started to send out the food en masse at 5:15, the residents had been waiting for close to half an hour. When all of the 117 people living at St. Matthew's were situated, the food was unceremoniously placed in front of them. There was a nurse in the room in case of a choking or other food-related accident. There were also at least four CNAs to assist those who could no longer cut their food or bring the fork to their mouth. There were always a few empty spaces, and some tables were missing up to three people because of illness or just not feeling well enough to take the trek down to the dining room. Sally observed all of this with a lump in her throat, as she thought that these people's lives didn't seem to amount to much anymore.

There was a strange silence while everyone was sitting, eating, staring. The silence was embedded somewhere in the staring. No one who resided here was talking, but there was a chattering of "Come on, Betty, open your mouth," or "John, you like cauliflower, come on, eat a little for me, please." It was not overly apparent that the staff had been trained about treating the elderly like adults and not like children, but Sally thought they must surely mean well.

The phone started ringing. The third floor was requesting Mary's plate be sent upstairs, as she wasn't up to going downstairs to the dining room tonight. The overhead speaker was squawking for one of the nurses to report to the dining room. So far there were only aides and no registered staff there in the event of a possible choking.

The kitchen aides knew not to place any food down until the nurse arrived, but they felt badly as people were hungry and the chicken was getting colder by the second under the rose-colored plastic plate cover.

After about thirty minutes, they were done. Their evening activity was over for another 23 hours. The first bunch that arrived started getting up and heading to the elevator. George didn't. He knew he couldn't just go up to that bedroom until 7 a.m. the next day. He walked, cane in hand, over to the lobby where he sat in front of the evening receptionist.

Carmelita knew George well. Their dialogue was familiar too.

"How was dinner, George?"

"Oh, you know, the same. I like the dessert usually."

"What was it today, George?"

"I don't know. Something chocolate, but I liked it. My wife used to make chocolate desserts. You know that?"

"You've told me that a few times."

"I have? Oh, gee, Carm, I'm sorry."

"Oh, no, I'm sorry. I didn't mean it like that. I just wanted you to know that I listen to you." Silence. "I like you, George."

Silence. Then, a tear slowly streamed down his face. He caught it with the back of his hand as soon as he could.

"I'm just so afraid I'll end up like the rest here. Every time you or one of the nursing folks tell me I've told them something, all I can think of is that I'm next and that it's happened to me. You are so young, Carm, you can't imagine, but it's a terrible feeling to live this long. And it's a worse feeling to look at these folks to see what I'll become next year, or maybe even next week. Gee, who knows, maybe it's tomorrow. What if I wake up tomorrow and don't know who George is anymore?"

"Oh, George, you'll always know who you are. You just have to look in the mirror and you'll know. Come downstairs here, find me, and I'll tell you."

"That's sweet, but I've heard the nurses say Frannie, before she died, went from being like me to being like the rest. She literally woke up, looked in the mirror, and screamed, 'Who the hell is that?'"

"Oh, Georgie, I hadn't heard that. Now just stop this nonsense."

As usual, by the time George made it upstairs, he was the last resident on the unit. At 6:30, he peeked in most of the bedrooms and observed that half his fellow inmates were already in bed or being put in bed. He calculated in his head that this was about twelve hours or half the day they're out of the way of the staff. He shuffled into his room. His roommate was already snoring. What now?

George was saying to himself, "This is my life now, life in a nursing home." He was ashamed, but less now that he was alone, and allowed more shameful tears to roll. He sat on the edge of his bed thinking again about those chocolate desserts. He wondered who made them and what sort of life they led. For the first time in his life, he regretted that he and his wife did not have children. When people suggested they should adopt children because it would ensure someone would be there for them when they were old, he was always first to tell them it didn't always work out that way. He knew friends whose children never bothered with them when they aged and needed the children to give back a bit. Plus, he would tell these people, "I am as healthy as a horse. I won't ever live in some goddamned nursing home." Now he thought, *Ha, I guess the last laugh was on me.*

Inner thoughts segued to vocal ones. "I guess I'd risk it. If I had to do it all over again, I would have had children. Maybe if I gave them everything and I still had to be sent here, they'd come visit me every night. Or maybe not?"

Silence. Undressing, shifting his tired old body into bed, then lights out. The silence of the third wave of rolling tears.

"George, wake up." Flo tried gently to wake George. It was already seven in the morning and George was always up by 6:30. Flo stopped abruptly when her arm brushed his and it was apparent he died in the night. Earlier in the night, she thought. As a registered nurse, Flo was allowed to call the time of death. Not wasting any time, she looked at her wristwatch and said aloud to no one, "Time of death: 7:03 a.m." She raised the sheet over his cold, dead body and left his room to document his passing on the chart.

Sally Cournan was asked later that morning to call the next of kin. His nephew through marriage lived in New Hampshire. He told Sally he wasn't sure he could get down to Boston to make arrangements and was it all right to do it by phone. Sally ended up calling the funeral director and making the arrangements. There would be no wake, and the nephew and a few cousins would gather for a funeral Mass on Saturday at 9 a.m. at the church. Only the cousins, Sally, Flo, and Carmelita made it to the church that morning.

Chapter 11: Nine o'clock Meeting

"OK, let's get this meeting going. It's already five after." It's the job of Director of Nursing, Kathy Foster, to start the daily staff meeting. Kathy is an old-school nurse with bad feet in a pair of orthopedic shoes and a gravelly voice that sounds as if it's been party to a carton a week for the past thirty years. Kathy always had the best intentions with patient care. She had her start in a tuberculosis ward at the city hospital, where she also earned her associate's in nursing and the sacred RN license. Only after a lifetime of staff nursing on acute care hospital wards did she finally give in and try her hand at an "administrative" nursing job.

The 9 a.m. meeting is a standard practice in every nursing home. It's the opportunity for all major department heads to gather each day to review the "house roster." All incidents, accidents, and other noteworthy events are reviewed, as well as clinical statuses that have changed or worsened. New admissions are discussed, and deaths are reported to the team as well.

The director of social services is there, as well as the administrator, director of rehab, director of admissions, reimbursement nurses, nurse unit managers, business office manager, and heads of plant, housekeeping, and laundry are there as well. The director of nursing leads the meeting. Michael and Sally were both representing social services this day because they needed to address concerns about the Jansen family.

"Marylou Zeglewski, Martha Lehman, and Lawrence Atwell are all now in poor condition. I expect them to die within the week. Mary Nolan and Tommy Patterson were both rushed to the hospital yesterday hours apart. Yesterday basically sucked," Kathy was saying as Paul interrupted her.

"Kathy, keep it clean, please."

"As I was saying, yesterday was a *banner* day. Finally, deaths: Ann Heavey, Irene Balkin and George, all three left us by noon yesterday."

"So, where does that bring census down to?" Maureen asked.

"Not good. Maureen, who's on the horizon?" Paul asked his admissions director. "Also, have you been back to the hospitals to market our rehab unit? If they don't know we are more than a nursing home, they won't send us the Medicare."

Sally couldn't control herself another minute. "People. We are talking about people, right? People who have Medicare as their insurance and who come here for a short-term re-hab stay are people, they are not the name of their insurance benefit. Furthermore, can I please remind you we are a nursing home through and through? That's what we do here, we provide 24-hour nursing for sick and elderly people who need skilled nursing care, and it becomes their home. We are not 'a rehab' as our so-called marketing material calls it. People who come here for a rehab stay do not have the Cadillac secondary insurance to supplement their Medicare, which is why they get their OT and PT here and not at a rehab hospital. I know these payments keep us afloat, but if we all become drones who eat, sleep, and drink the final equations that help us to make money and pay bills, then we won't have anyone to take care of because people will stop coming here. Or stop getting *sent* here, as the case may be. I am sorry for—"

Paul cut her off abruptly. "Sally, I appreciate your passion and am glad you're part of the team here at St. Matthew's. It's the work social services has done over the years that has helped our reputation climb so high. However, I must disagree when it comes to knowing the bottom line equations that make this place work. The answer is yes, you do need to know how it works. So does Bob over here. It doesn't matter if you are in plant and laundry or in social services, why wouldn't you want to know what the business office, admissions director, and I go through to make sure you all get a paycheck?"

"Well, I don't think reducing all the residents down to a payment category is what gets us all a paycheck. I thought it was about providing a pleasant, home-like environment with quality nursing care, healthy food, and other medical and clinical care as needed."

"Sally, you really think that's how we look at the residents? I don't. I know this is their last stop, and I want to make sure we make it as pleasant a stay as possible. Yes, Medicaid and Medicare pay us a daily rate based on their acuity and their nursing needs. We aren't going to lie and state on the claims submissions that they need fewer of our services and support than they do. Reimbursement is an important function here, and we should all be aware of how it gets calculated. And you're absolutely right that we should care about the quality nursing care and healthy food, but I can't meet payroll and purchase food without the reimbursement attached to every person in a bed here." Paul pontificated all this clearly, with just a hint of preachiness.

Sally could only offer, "It is what it is and we'll just have to continue the dialogue and respect each other's perspective, but that's why I'm a social worker and you're not."

"It's not easy running a nursing home."

"Facility. You are running a nursing facility. That's the best the reimbursement can come up with—for a facility. It is clearly not a home and probably hasn't been since the late eighties."

Paul walked out, got to his office, stormed in, and slammed the door shut. He looked at the picture of one of his favorite residents from seven years ago. Alice's picture, taken in the middle of an Irish concert planned by the activities department, was still perched on his desk. The picture was there to remind him why he got into this business. As Paul picked it up, he was suddenly engulfed in a tidal wave of emotions. When did it go wrong? When did it really change? Was Sally right, was it the late eighties when Congress enacted the Nursing Home Reform Act? "Actually, I think it was when the psych hospitals were all shut down by the Republican administration of the early nineties. When we were forced to take in all the middle-aged mentally ill people who had nowhere to go, regardless of whether they even needed skilled nursing. Is that when the downfall began? It sure wasn't my fault," Paul said to no one in particular.

The next day, the 9 a.m. meeting started with the usual litany of who was admitted, who was taken to the ER, who had died, or who was close to dying. The best part of the meeting was the incident report. The director of nursing, with Sally and Michael from social services, took turns sharing who was behaving badly, hitting roommates, trying to escape, and there was also the daily listing of falls and subsequent reactive measures to try and ensure no future falls for Ethel. It was not the most uplifting meeting, really, and was rather depressing. It was a daily face-the-truth while they were spinning their wheels trying to do something to rectify it among a sea of regulations, family complaints, staff issues, resident complaints, and other issues. All the while, the corporate suits were counting every dollar of reimbursement and trying to cut expenses and payroll to make the P & L go from red to black. Every day, the team sat around a conference room table talking about the folks they were trying desperately to keep safe and to medicate to keep them alive. If not, the staff was accused of some degree of assisted suicide. There were still falls, accidents, strokes, suspected or real abuse, and other incidents that punctuated every day.

Peggy finished the meeting with her plans to screen patients at the local acute care hospitals to bring the census back up as close as possible to the facility's capacity of 123. Peggy assured Paul and others she was pretty sure she'd get a hip replacement from the Boston Medical Center and a recent MI survivor for some cardiac rehab from New England Medical Center. The hip replacement had no living relatives in the area, so she might be a shoe-in for an eventual long-term stay!

It was just another day in the life of running a business which just happened to have human beings as the cog in the wheel. Tomorrow would be another roll call.

Chapter 12: Who Are You?

Sally was ruminating about her work and what she'd chosen for a career when she realized that the problem with Alzheimer's was that the individual not only forgets who they are, the individual forgets who you are. If no one is there to remind them, they fade into the background of the wallpaper. *It's really the problem with most people at St. Matthew's,* she thought. *How do we expect them to communicate with us when there is no frame of reference for them as a starting point in the conversation?*

Sally remembered the countless times one of the residents had asked a nurse, a family member, or her, "Who are you?" or "Why are you here?" And another frequent question was, "Where are we going now?" She thought about how hard it must be for the person interacting with the resident. Where do they go with this? As Sally well knew, they typically went to her office. Some cried and others denied, while some families used transference and blamed the nursing home for all their loved one's problems.

As Sally walked past the activities room, she heard Margaret ask the activities assistant to get her "that thing over there by that machine thing." Lea, the day shift CNA, went over to the microwave to get Margaret the cup of tea she had placed in there thirty seconds earlier. Terry Flynn, a twenty-year-old working as an assistant in the activities department, asked Lea how she knew what Margaret wanted.

"Terry, check out the non-verbals. These go last, you know. Don't rely on her to give you full sentences every time she is trying to ask you for something. Really, how long you have been here anyway?"

"I don't know, six months? Why? What did I do?"

"You didn't do anything at all," Lea continued, "you just didn't know how to interpret what was going on, what she wanted. It's all right, considering her daughter didn't know how to either. That's why she's here. The more Margaret's daughter didn't understand—or bother to learn how to under-stand—what her mother was trying to express when words were failing her, the more Margaret got frustrated and gave up. The less Margaret communicated, the more her daughter was increasingly convinced she was losing it and had some awful disease like the often mentioned Alzheimer's. The more 'daughter' started treating 'mother' like a memory-impaired idiot, the more 'mother' started acting like one, a learned help-lessness type of behavior. It didn't take long before the mani-festation of this helplessness was daughter coming home from work to see that Margaret hadn't eaten anything all day. Before you know it, she comes home from work one day to the smell of feces. Yes, indeed, Margaret couldn't remember where or how to get to the bathroom. After a little bit of scolding, there were tears and then the inevitable conversation."

"Terry, it probably went something like this." Lea pro-ceeded to imitate the roles of Margaret and her daughter for Terry.

"Daughter: Mother, what would you think of spending your days with friends and not all by yourself here?

Margaret: Where are my friends?

Daughter: Well, they will be at your new home, nice, new friends and lots of nice women your age.

Margaret: I'm going to a new home with all my friends? What's wrong with my old home? What's wrong with their old homes?

Daughter: Mother, this is your old home . . . I mean current home. You haven't had an old home since 38 Dakota Street.

Margaret: Will my friends from Dakota Street be at this new home? Is it a full circle of life type of thing? I think maybe this *is* the way to go . . .

Daughter: Oh, that's *exactly it*, Mother. Some of the girls from the Dakota Street neighborhood and girls from State Teacher's College, and some of the girls from bridge club too. They'll all be there."

Margaret, of course, was somewhat more interested, or conciliatory anyway. The following Monday morning, she was officially a resident at St. Matthew's Nursing Care Center. A member of the St. Matthew's neighborhood or community? She wasn't sure.

Margaret spent the first few hours looking out the window to see some semblance of what Dakota Street might look like today. Nope. Next, she looked through her doorway to the hallway, to see all the old friends pass by. They were surely bound to show up any minute now. They didn't. "There's something wrong here. I just know my daughter wouldn't lie to me. There is something missing or I'm having a dream—a bad dream. I'll just wait until I wake up."

Margaret woke up at 6 a.m., and when she tried to get out of bed, it was to the sound of an unfamiliar voice saying, "You need to stay in bed, Mrs. Baldwin, until the next shift comes on. There just aren't enough of us."

What's a girl to do? So of course she got up. What does that mean anyway— "not enough of us"? Not enough of whom? What's a "shift" anyway? And somewhere in the middle of all this, she thought to herself, *Where am I?* Not thinking that she really was somewhere else, Margaret slipped and fell since her footing wasn't yet steady in this unfamiliar place supposedly known as her new home.

Five or ten minutes later, a new CNA named Pauline happened to walk past room 309 when she saw Margaret Baldwin squirming on the floor, looking like a drug addict writhing through a withdrawal.

"Ma'am, why are you on the floor? What happened? Let me get you up."

"Stop right there!" yelled Flo as she heard some of the commotion. "Do not touch her. That's a good way to break her back or something else. Now move along and tell Dottie at the nurses' station."

"Mrs. Baldwin, this is Flo and I'm your nurse. Can you hear me?" Flo started checking her pulse and any movement in her carotid artery with a finger on each of these areas to make sure the fall didn't kill her. That would have really sucked, in Flo's estimation. Not only would it involve calling time of death and all the documentation that goes with pronouncing one of these people dead, but the incident report would have to be filled out, the Department of Public Health would have to be called due to the accidental nature of the death, and worst of all, DPH would come knocking and ask Flo countless questions about how she could have avoided the fall. With forty residents to worry about first thing in the morning between first round of meds and breakfast being served, Flo wondered how the hell she was supposed to ensure no one slipped and fell.

Flo checked Margaret's pulse and after determining she was truly alive, asked if her back hurt. Margaret just stared into space. Flo placed her fingers on the lowest vertebrae and asked again, "Do you feel anything now? Do you feel any pain, Mrs. Baldwin?"

"I don't know who you are and where I am, nor do I know what you're asking me."

"OK, this sounds a little better," Flo muttered somewhat under her breath. "OK, Mrs. Baldwin, I'm going to start lifting you back to your bed now. Just tell me when it hurts, and see if you can try to help me by bearing some weight on my shoulder."

All Margaret could think about was why she was here and who Flo was and why Flo was picking her up off the floor.

"Yes, goddamn it, it hurts! It hurts like hell! What if I fall on the floor and have to lean on your shoulder? I don't know if I am going to die of pneumonia. I think this is a nursing home, and this is how and where I'll die. No one knows me anymore or will ever find me here. Help!"

"I *am* helping you, Mrs. Baldwin. That's why you're here, so nurses can help you with some of your care needs and give you some medical attention."

"My what—care needs? Oh, never mind. Thanks anyway, sweetie." And to no one at all, Margaret Baldwin muttered under her breath, "Whoever you are."

Something about this incident and the interaction with Flo affected Margaret and woke her up to the fact she was not going back to the home she shared with her daughter. She silently cursed her daughter and wished she had never given her so much love and attention.

Chapter 13: Family Night

It was a gray, rainy Thursday night, and Bridget Baldwin was fighting traffic on Dorchester Avenue to get to St. Matthew Nursing Care Center. The invitation had arrived in the mail last week.

Meet the St. Matthew's Administration and Nurse Management Team
Ask Questions, Get Answers
Thursday, March 19th 7:00 – 8:30 p.m.

She still didn't know what was compelling her to drive over there on a day that didn't begin with an "S." She kept wondering, *It is what it is, right? I mean, you can't make these places any better, and I spent a lot of time deciding which would be the best one for Mom. It doesn't seem perfect, but I always tell the nurse, Flo, what I need for Mom or what I think she would want if she were still able to say what it is she wants and needs. Why am I going here tonight? It's a Catholic nursing home, and there's a chapel. I hear Mom goes to Mass every Wednesday and Saturday. It doesn't get any better. I suppose I could ask about the staffing and how they decide how many nurses and nurses' aides are scheduled for each shift. I mean, sometimes, well, I guess most of the time, I smell shit when I visit Mom. But then again, it is a nursing home, and they can't possibly keep up with that many people constantly messing their pants. It is a little horrifying when I think about it, that a grown woman who worked hard all her life and put her quarters into the Social Security system isn't given enough back to keep her from having to hope someone has enough time in her shift to remember when she needs to be taken to the toilet. Or at the very least, when they notice—smell with their damned noses—that the accident has occurred, they have the common sense to ensure her decency.*

Bridget was suddenly jolted back to earth by the sounds of a police siren. She pulled over and rolled down her window.

The officer asked Bridget, "What's the hurry, ma'am?"

She handed the apparently nice black police officer her license and registration and mumbled something about her mother's nursing home and wanting to get there on time to make a good impression, to show she really does care about her mother. And to top it off she said, "I want to complain about those lazy CNAs."

"My wife, Marie St. Jean, is a CNA there. She'll be at the meeting. Tell her Greg says he hopes she works harder for the ungrateful old folks' families."

Bridget's day was not getting any better anytime soon.

"Oh, sir, I mean 'officer,' I am so sorry, and I meant no disrespect. Um, such a coincidence . . . I just mean that I want to show I care and I don't take them for granted."

"Who *are* them? People like my wife?"

"Oh, no, officer. I mean the administration positions. You know, the director of nursing, the social workers, and the administrator. I can tell they all think the same of us family members. They think we just dumped them there and that we don't care and couldn't be bothered with our own mothers and fathers. Can you believe they really think we are too busy in our own lives to make room for caring for the very people who gave us life?"

"Ma'am, I believe that answer is a qualified 'yes.'"

"Excuse me, officer? What did you say? Did you just tell me you believe the answer to my diatribe is a YES? Really? No, reeeeeally? Why would they think that? They see many of us every, well, almost every Saturday and Sunday. I know some families I've met go on weeknights, too. I mean, they must know with the traffic around this city we can't possibly get there more than a couple of times a week. Right?"

"Are you asking me, ma'am?"

"Well, yes, officer. I am asking you."

"Marie tells me that when she is with a person, another human being who needs care and assistance, it's for about 50 hours per week. Well, that is, 50 of the person's 168 hours, or less than a third of their waking hours, in which you can begin to understand who they are, what they are, and what they are going through. It comes close to empathy. Marie and her colleagues, cliché sounding or not, become your mother's family. They are there to put them to bed and the first person they see when they wake up in the morning. They're there to bring them to the toilet, and there to change them when they couldn't guess the exact time the patient was going to need the toilet. Bottom line, ma'am, is that you can choose differently."

"Choose what?"

"Why, you can choose to suck up the traffic, or spend less time on your gardening, or make a couple fewer home cooked meals for your husband and take those new hours in your week and give them to your mother."

"I'll just take the ticket, please, and a little less of your pontification and telling me how to be a daughter to someone who barely recognizes me."

Bridget walked into the family meeting. It was held in the nursing home's activities room. The set-up resembled something like an AA meeting, complete with the aluminum coffee urn and paper cups. Members of the management staff were sitting on folding chairs at the front of the room and answering questions from the audience of family members. Bridget was told she missed the "presentations" about all the positive changes they were making at St. Matthew, but she stayed around to see what she could learn anyway.

When she saw Peggy, she beelined over to her corner of the room to have a word with one of the few familiar and trusting faces she knew. This was all still pretty scary for her, and at least Peggy helped her with the paperwork when she first brought her mother here.

"Hi, Bridget, I'm so glad you joined us tonight. Did you get any coffee or soda?"

"I'm all set. I just hate being here. I know that sounds awful, but I am flooded with feelings I just can't control when I'm here. I hate the smell of urine and the sound of these people yelling or crying, or begging for someone to say hello or pay attention to them. Peggy, it's just horrible. It is!" Bridget let out a small sob as she fell into the nearest chair.

"What's *horrible* exactly?"

"*It* is."

"What is 'it,' though?"

"It's me. I'm horrible. No, I'm not, but it's in me."

Peggy drew her into a slight hug. "Bridget, you're right, it's not you. You're a good daughter who is trying her best, or the best you know how to do in a situation where you had no training, nor did you see it coming to prepare yourself. You're feeling what almost every son or daughter does when they admit their parent to a nursing home. It's nothing more than guilt. You feel guilty. I'm sorry if that's plain and simple, but that's what it is. I haven't dealt with a family here in almost seventeen years who didn't display their guilt. Christ, some wear it on their sleeves. Many blame *us*. It's normal, and you have to stop beating yourself up."

"I'll take that coffee now. A little Kahlua too. Just kidding!"

Chapter 14: The First Fall

Lillian and Max had just returned from 8 a.m. Mass. They typically went to the 11, but their granddaughter's eighth grade graduation was at noon today so they were forced to alter their schedule. As usual, with no less than four bathroom trips during the night and the inevitable inability to fall back to sleep after each pit stop, Max and Lillian were exhausted.

Max is eighty-two and Lillian is a spry seventy-eight. They still live in their own home—a three-story townhouse condominium—and proudly make all their own meals, manage the cleaning, laundry, and grocery shopping. This shopping is accomplished via the 2007 Pontiac they recently bought brand new. Neither Max nor Lillian pretends for a second they aren't feeling the ravages of the years or that they don't move a little slower than they used to. In fact, recently they both admitted to one another that their memory isn't quite what it used to be. Dr. Richards prescribed Aricept for both of them, but unfortunately each forgets or chooses not to take it most days. So the bathroom shelf has the sharpest memory in town.

Max tells Lillian they should lie down for a while or he'll never make it to the graduation, or through it anyway. Lillian tells Max she'll rub his feet to help put him to sleep. Soon after he falls asleep, Lillian decides to get up to putter. She stands too quickly, falls back on the couch, and without pause tries again. This time she completely loses her balance and falls at a diagonal angle right onto the glass coffee table.

Max rises immediately and screams, "What the hell just happened?"

"Please don't scream at me. I think I've broken something. I can't get up."

"How the hell did you do this? What if you did break something, how will we get to the graduation? Jaaaysus!"

"I hit the coffee table. I don't know how. If I knew how, it wouldn't have happened, don't you think? Really, dear, I just need to lie back down. It will be fine."

Two days later, Max still can't get Lillian to get off the couch except to go to the bathroom, and that is done in the most precarious manner. He started cooking all the meals and bringing them to her at the couch. When the pain seemed to be getting worse, it finally dawned on Max to ask if she would like to go to the local emergency room. Lillian wasn't sure she really needed to and instead suggested that another day of rest should do the trick.

The next day, Pat Jensen, the neighbor across the way, knocked on the door. Pat was a retired registered nurse who had worked in a hospital for thirty-five years. Pat asked Max why the car hadn't moved in a few days and whether everything was all right with him and Lillian. He filled her in on what happened on Sunday.

Pat walked into the living room, saw her friend, an ashen, weak looking woman she barely recognized, and immediately exclaimed, "Max, we have to get Lillian to the hospital! She can't just stay on this couch after a major fall that happened three days ago."

"Pat, I am so sorry, I just didn't know. She kept telling me she was going to get better. Please don't think I'm a bad husband."

"Oh, Max, please. No, no, no! I'm not saying that. I am just as much to blame for not coming over sooner."

"Where do we go from here? What am I going to do?"

"Well, just come with me. We're going to the emergency room and see what they say at the hospital. OK?"

"OK, Pat. I don't know what I'd do if you hadn't come over."

Pat asked Lillian where the pain was, how she felt now, and if she understood that they had to get her to the hospital.

"Let's go," were Pat's last words before they headed out the door.

The hospital admitted Lillian, and she stayed for four days before the discharge planner, Carol, started discussions with Max about some of the very good nursing homes in the area.

Max asked Carol why she didn't think he could take Lillian home.

Carol asked Max in return, "If the neighbor Pat hadn't happened to stop by, what was your plan to seek medical attention for your wife?" Carol certainly presented this question in the most gracious and unthreatening manner she could muster. Her fifteen years of hospital social services work cultivated this probing approach to getting family to realize that the long-term options were few.

"I still don't understand why I can't just take my wife home when she's ready. Don't fifty-five years of taking care of each other stand for something? Just because she fell and broke something doesn't change anything that we have together. All these years . . . you, you know what I mean, don't you?"

"Mr. Fischer, I hope you know how much I am in awe of your marriage and partnership. I think it is so sweet you've taken care of each other as much as you have after your kids have gone. I especially know this gets harder with the onset of age and the physical issues that accompany our getting older. And, I mean, really, you are so good about what you are doing and how you go about doing it, but what I am really trying to say is that, well, you know, it is hard to take care of someone who may have a cognitive deficit. You may also be experiencing the same type of medical issue. So, I am just trying to tell you tha—"

"Stop, please miss, just stop. I don't know what you are saying. It feels like doublespeak and is confusing the bejesus out of me, but I think I've gotten a feeling for the gist of it. Are you asking me if I am with it, competent enough, for my own wife to come back to our home? Is this what you're asking me?"

"Well, yes sir, I am."

"Do you understand that I have three daughters, a son and a good friend who is a nurse and a neighbor all bundled together? Do you understand that, Miss Social Worker?"

"I do. I do. But first, do you know, I mean to say, do you realize, how upsetting and difficult this is for me? After fifteen years of discharge planning, I still have pains—even nightmares—over telling a spouse or a loved one they have to consider a nursing home."

"I am so sorry to be one more difficult 'loved one' conversation notch on your belt. I guess you took me for a fool. Not only am I not a fool, but I am keen—yes, keen! So, without really talking about it, I mean explaining it, you were just telling me my wife was going to be institutionalized? Really?"

"Oh, no, Mr. Fischer, I don't know where you got that idea. This state doesn't institutionalize. You seem to be stuck—I mean, focused—on an antiquated term and paradigm for what is now a loving and caring facility—I mean, home. They are called nursing homes now, and you are very mistaken about my intent."

"Miss, can we just get past this? I *am* taking my wife home as soon as she's ready, and she is not going to any nursing fa-cil-i-tee." Max put a lot of emphasis on the last syllable.

"Back in the day, when my grandparents were starting to fail, my mother and father—God rest their souls too—took in both of my grandparents. There was no question about it and no social workers at hospitals telling us we can't take care of our kin. We got by and figured it out. And you know what? Well, I'll tell you what. People died in their own home, in their own beds with their families by their side. What changed? What's so different now that you don't trust people to take their own wife home? Are we suddenly less equipped to do that?"

"Mr. Fischer, much has changed, but many things stay the same. I am sure your mother was taking care of her parents at an age somewhat younger than your current age. You are trying to take care of a frail, aging woman when you are eighty-two years old yourself."

"Trying? Let's get something straight here, I am not trying to do anything. I *am* very sure I will continue to take care of my wife at home with the help of my daughters and our neighbor. I am not stupid, and I am not saying it will be easy or that I won't rely on a good deal of help, but I am telling you this will happen this way. Do I need to ask for your supervisor or are you going to start respecting the wishes of an old man? Old, but still capable."

"Well, Mr. Fischer, I suppose we can see how it goes, sort of like a trial. A trial for you and Lillian. Mrs. Fischer, that is. I'll set up a discharge planning meeting. I will need you there, as well as any family members or other significant people in Lillian's caregiving circle. I will also be inviting

the local Visiting Nurse Association. You see, I will be asking them to assess Lillian's need for personal care and skilled
nursing visits."

"Wait. It's standard practice for you to refer visiting nurses
and aides to people who are leaving your hospital. Right?"

"Well, yes, of course. I don't understand what's wrong
with accepting a little bit of help."

"No, no, no. This time you're not getting what I'm saying.
Since you send your patients back to their homes with assistance, then this is clearly one of your practices. I was convinced for the past thirty minutes or so I had no option but to
sign my wife over to one of those stinking nursing facilities.
What am I missing here?"

"I always speak with the medical team first to ascertain
whether the patient needs 24-hour nursing or whether a few
hours a day of assistance is enough to keep her safe and
healthy. We have initially assessed Mrs. Fischer as needing
around-the-clock nursing care, which is what nursing homes
provide. We didn't think you would be able to take care of
her every medical need and her activities of daily living. I'm
sorry, what I mean is, will you be able to get her into bed at
night and help her in and out of the tub or shower? And can
you stand by the stove cooking her meals at least twice a
day? I am sorry if it sounds like I think you might not be able
to, but I just need to lay out the situation for you."

"Lay out the situation? I know what my house is like, and
I know who my wife is and what I need to do for her. I don't

know, however, what you mean when you speak at me. I mean, to me."

"OK, Mr. Fischer. Let's set up a home visit. Can you agree to that? One of either the physical therapists or occupational therapists will come to your home and do an assessment of its safety and feasibility for Mrs. Fischer's recuperative needs. What do you say?"

"I'll do whatever it takes for you to believe me. I guess I just never thought it would come to this." The hospital social worker was shuffling papers and therefore missed seeing this eighty-two-year-old man suppress the tears emerging from his tired, sad, gray-brown eyes.

A few days later, the home evaluation substantiated the social worker's suspicions that the house wasn't elder-impaired proof. Mrs. Fischer was admitted to St. Matthew's three days later.

Chapter 15: The Visitor

Graham Nolan moved back to Boston after finishing his PhD at Berkeley in California. He hadn't lived in Boston for almost ten years and wasn't about to go back to West Roxbury, the westernmost part of the city that looked and felt like a suburb, or to any other part of the city that reminded him of home. He settled into South Boston, the original Irish section of the city, where a man with a name like Nolan would easily be welcome. While Graham was stacking initials on the end of his name out in California, two of his three surviving grandparents had died.

It was always too expensive, or difficult anyway, to get back to Boston for funerals. Besides, the one in the casket doesn't even know you're there, so he assuaged his guilt by praying to the "spirit" of the recently deceased and reflecting on their life and how it had impacted his. His parents were *not* young adults losing a parent and most likely spoke the tired old adage "It's a blessing in disguise" when one of their parents died. So nobody bothered to chastise him or remark on his missing the funerals.

Graham's mom called him a few days after he settled into his apartment on West Seventh near K Street.

"You're not calling me for dinner already, Ma? I just want to settle in, see some old friends from high school, and maybe even—sit tight, Ma—see what the local bar scene is like."

"Oh, honey, I don't want you hanging around the 'gin mills' of Southie. But that's not the reason I called. I don't think your father told you that Gram Nolan was put in St. Matthew's recently. And it is actually walking distance from your new home. We just thought you'd want to stop by."

"You what? You put Gram in a fucking, I'm sorry, I mean a godforsaken nursing home? Ma, she's the only one left. Why the fuck did you go and do that? There's no one who could have helped you with her? What about Aunt Margaret or Uncle Donald or my useless sister, Kathleen? No one could step up to the plate and say, 'Hey, let's not throw another one of our elder relatives in a fuckin' shit-hole?' I mean really. Is this how our family functions?"

"Graham, calm yourself down. We don't speak that way and you certainly will not speak to your mother that way. PhD or no PhD, California living or no California living, that's not how we Nolans speak. And don't give me that 'I don't live under your roof' nonsense. I don't care. You are my son, and I am the mother, and that's how it will always be."

"Wait. Stop. I'm sorry, I'm just in shock here."

She continued scolding her adult son. "I only have a high school diploma, and I sure as heck don't speak like I'm from the gutter."

"Ma, Ma, settle down. I'm sorry. I didn't mean to curse. I am just so taken aback at the changes. I left over ten years ago and we had both your parents and Gram Nolan, and I come back to Grandma and Grandpa Curran dead and now I have to deal with Gram Nolan in St. Matthew's. I don't know how I can see her there."

"Well, you can. You *can* see her there. It's not pleasant, but it will mean the world to her and, Graham, it's not about you, it's about an old demented lady who needs some small measure of comfort to get through every day. So I can expect you there tomorrow, right!" It was *not* a question.

"Tomorrow" took about seven or eight days. One Wednesday night after work, Graham took the trek down the hill from his apartment over to St. Matthew's to see his grandmother.

As he walked up the hill, the past came flooding over him like it was yesterday. *"Honey, let me give you some more beef. You're a growing boy, with all that football you play and running around that track all the time, you need all the protein you can get."*

"Thanks, Gram. You don't have to fuss so much for me. I'm a visitor here and you're gonna go broke spending all your pension money on food for me."

"You're my grandson, Graham Nolan, you are not a visitor. And there hasn't been a time you've been here where you didn't cut my grass or shovel my drive. Why wouldn't I share my food with you, honey?"

"I know, Gram. I just meant to show my gratefulness— I mean, gratitude—better English, right Gram? I just feel badly because you were widowed so young and have so little money. I just, I just want you to know I would do anything for you and I, well, you know, I love you."

She rested her hand on his and gave him a smile that spoke more than a thousand words. Graham held back a tear or three and sprang up to do the dishes.

He was almost at the front door of this very large brick edifice that was called St. Matthew's, technically "St. Matthew, the Apostle Manor," but known to all in the community as "St. Matthew's." The lump in his throat was growing. As he reached for the front door, some strange hold took over his body and Graham suddenly found himself walking—no, actually sprinting—in the opposite direction.

He was racing back down the hill away from the nursing home as quickly as he possibly could when he tripped and fell on the curb. When he gathered his composure, Graham stopped. His thoughts vacillated between telling himself to breathe, think, and stop to question why he was doing this. *This isn't the end of the world, just because my grandmother ended up in a nursing home. People before me have dealt with this, if not more. Why can't I? My mom has to deal with her own mother being in this place. I can deal with my grandmother being in this place. It's Catholic, it's gotta be better than most of those shit-holes that pass for nursing homes. I'm sure it's good. The nuns will be there, praying with Gram and making sure she has all the comforts of home. Ma would not put her just any place. It's St. Matthew's, after all. I can do this. I can walk in that place.*

With that, Graham headed back up the hill. Despite the trepidation, he walked with an air of determination in his stride.

Three minutes later he was at the front door of the nursing home. He walked in fully prepared to be greeted with an odor of stale urine. That didn't happen. He walked past a vignette of furniture arranged in a half-hearted semi-circle, with an end table, lamp, and various doilies to make the old ladies feel at home. Overhead was a Home Depot chandelier, and at their feet was a nice HomeGoods faux Oriental rug. No smell of urine and no one screaming, "Get me out of here!" Graham walked past this area, headed to the receptionist's desk, and asked the attendee for Mrs. Nolan's room number. After signing the register and sanitizing his hands from the sanitizer dispenser, Graham headed to the elevator to move forward with his date with destiny. The breathing helped.

Why am I here? Oh, yeah, cuz they dumped my grandma here. And why did we—I mean my mother—do that? What the fuck, why did this have to happen to her and where was I to stop it? What the fuck? OK, OK, just breathe. Oh fuck, the elevator is opening. It's not the fourth floor yet. OK, is this nurse going to ask me questions? Will she know I'm a psycho case right now? Please, God, get me out of this and just let it end. Let her not really be here or, God forbid, let her be dead. Yeah, she died in her sleep last night, and I do not have to see her living like this.

"Sir, are you OK?" Sheila Sullivan had just gotten in the elevator to head down to see the director of nursing, who was doing rounds on the fourth floor, when she was greeted by this very handsome wreck of a human being.

"Yes, ma'am, I am just a little nervous about seeing my grandmother here for the first time."

"What makes you nervous about seeing your own grandmother? Haven't you seen her in a while?"

"No, I mean, yes, ma'am, it's been just a couple of years, but I haven't seen her here—here in a nursing home, that is. I am just a little shaken by the thought of it."

"By the thought of what?" After a pause in their dialogue, she continued. "You're very sweet to care about her so much, but why are you shaken by the thought of her living here? I'm a little insulted—and I certainly shouldn't feel that way, but what kind of statement does this make about all the caregivers here who are doing their best to give your grandmother a nice, clean home with round-the-clock nursing care? What about the CNAs who work horrible shifts for typically ten to eleven dollars per hour? How should they feel about your so-called view of their chosen profession?"

"Miss—not sure I can read your name tag—oh, Sullivan, I am very sorry. I was just thinking about myself and having my own pity party. I should have thought about the bigger picture. I am sorry. I mean that. I don't criticize what people do for a living, and it actually seems very praiseworthy. I know some people—many people, I guess—need to live here and need caring people like the CNAs I have seen. It's just that people like my mother shouldn't rush to put their parents in a nursing home. That is, not until they absolutely have to. That's all. It's a place to go when there is no one left to take care of you and nowhere left for you to go. It shouldn't be for people who still have options. That's all I have to say on this topic." Graham looked exhausted by the time he finished giving this stranger his thoughts on parent-rearing.

"So, what were your grandmother's options?"

"Well, that's easy, Miss Sullivan. Her options were to either move in with my mother or have my mother provide home care people to look in on my grandmother when my mother wouldn't have been available."

"OK, first of all, this 'Miss Sullivan' nonsense has got to go. My name is Sheila. Secondly, a few questions. How many hours a week does your mom work? How many hours a week were you prepared—you are the one, I assume—to pay for the home care workers? When the home care had to leave and your mother wasn't home from work, then what? And I have to ask you what happens every evening and all day long on Saturdays and Sundays?"

He was rendered a little bit speechless, and after many iterations of stammering in an attempt to interrupt Nurse Sheila, Graham finally said, "Well, um, I think people just figure these things out. You do what you have to do, right? What about *your* grandparents? Were you lucky enough that they had cancer in their fifties or had a heart attack or stroke in their sixties? If they made it to seventy, did you start facing these issues?"

"Mister, I'm sorry, but you have your priorities a little fucked up. Yes, I just used that word in a professional setting, and yes, my *mother* did actually die from cancer when she was only fifty-nine. You call that fucking lucky? Really? No, *really*, I was lucky at nineteen that my mother suffered a gruesome and painful death from ovarian cancer? Really? I'd have her 'suffering' here as an eighty or ninety-year-old woman any old day. I really don't have too much more to say to you, other than the fact that she's down in room 314."

She was sitting by the window, yes, actually in a rocking chair. The light from the large window was shining on her weathered but still beautiful face. Her twin bed was adorned with a hand-sewn, homey-looking bedspread. Her bureau was lined with photographs of Graham, his sister, his various cousins, aunts and uncles, and his parents were at the center of many framed photographs. Gram wore a lovely lime green sweater over a lightweight print dress of yellows and greens. Her hair was neatly coiffed, and her feet were resting on a cute, little, old-fashioned step stool. She may or may not have been resting when she looked up and smiled at the sight of her favorite grandson.

Holding back the tears to the best of his ability and using his shirtsleeves to wipe the ones that had already trickled down his face, Graham approached her chair in a stilted gait, as if rushing toward her would have caused her undue stress. Or possibly caused stress to him. They embraced, he sobbed, and she cried, just a bit.

"Gram, I am so sorry. I don't know what happened with time or why I am finally here, uh, I mean, why it took me so long to finally get here. I, I just wish that—"

She cut him off quickly. "Wish that *what*? What is every-one always feeling so guilty about? Just say hello and that you are glad to see me. Graham, darling, is that so hard?"

"Of course I am glad to see you. I just wanted you to know I wish I could have helped or done something for you. Some-thing that would have prevented . . ."

Gram was feeling just a little annoyed with this particular reunion and asked, "Prevent what? Do what for me? Such as? What were you going to do for me, my dear? I like it here. I know where everything is. I get three squares a day, someone to give me all my medicine. You know, dear, that I was taking all the wrong doses and sometimes not taking my medicine at all. I couldn't keep up with the house, the chores, the bill-paying. You know, dear, I forgot to pay the taxes after a while."

"Gram, how could you forget property taxes?"

"I know. It *does* sound silly. I got confused with the con-cept of the mortgage being discharged and thinking it meant everything was done—except utilities I guess. I don't know. It's all so far away now."

"Far away, Gram, are you kidding? That was about eigh-teen months or possibly two years ago."

"Oh, no dear, that was twenty years ago when I stopped paying those taxes. I never could keep up with that farm-house and all those acres of land."

"Acres of land? Gram, you had a tiny little house in South Boston. A mile from here—a mile up the street from this nursing home!"

"Nursing home? Oh, Thomas, you have lost it. This is a resort I paid a lot of money to belong to. A nursing home? You poor thing. What happened to you?"

"Gram, this is St. Matthew's Nursing Home. Look right here, on the wall. See the bulletin board—it says St. Matthew's Nursing Home, room 314B. That's this room, and your bed here is considered 'bed B.' This is where you live."

"Oh, honey, I need to rest now. Thanks so much for visiting me here, and I do hope you come back soon. It's always so fun to see all you kids out here in the country."

"But I just got here. I thought we'd catch up a little. Really, Gram, I don't have to leave yet. And I am *Graham.*"

"I know you don't, honey, but I'm tired. Come back soon. Good night, dear. Love to your parents. And I *know* your name," she added with much emphasis.

Graham started praying, "Please, God, tell me this isn't happening. She is really *gone,* isn't she? Do I placate her or help her know the truth and the reality that is today?" Graham finally stammered out, "Gram, my dad died nine or ten years ago. You remember, you sat next to Ma and me at his funeral over at St. Luke's."

"I remember when they built St. Luke's. I was there. You were too. You were maybe ten or eleven. You were the first priest there, weren't you? In fact, I still remember your first Mass. Everyone was there, even the Mayor of Boston and his wife. I do believe Rose Kennedy was there too. You remember, don't you, dear?"

After a moment that felt like an eternity, a few deep breaths, and some major tongue biting to hold back his tears, Graham's need for composure and a dose of reality was rendered useless in this dialogue. His recent—five-minute recent, that is—surprise that his pride and joy *was not* gone from this world faded lightning fast, and now there was nothing left but a canvas of confusion that mixed events by centuries, people, and facts. *What do I do now?* was all he could focus on while he smiled and feigned amazement at the Kennedy matriarch being in the same church at the same time with his grandmother almost eighty years ago. Interestingly enough, Graham was alleged to have been there too, despite his not being alive just yet, and as a priest, no less.

Somewhere in this zany dialogue, he said, "Oh, Gram, I didn't know St. Luke's was built less than forty years ago. It looks so much older. I wonder if you're thinking of St. Mark's up on the Avenue? And you know, there were thoughts—or I think it was my mother's hopes and dreams—that I would become a priest, but as we all recall I chose against that vocation while still in high school. It must get confusing with so many grandchildren, nieces, nephews, great-nieces, and great-nephews. Actually, didn't Cousin Shirley have a son who became a priest? Or was it a Christian Brother? I think he teaches at Christian Brothers Academy, right?"

Instead of a shifting back into reality, Graham was answered with, "What time are we going to the restaurant? I know we're heading out before five because the Mass is first, and then we're all eating shortly afterward. Did you say all your children are coming? I know my mother wants to see all our children at the party tonight, dear."

"Gram, please, you have to listen to me. I am not a priest, and I do not have children, and there is no Mass or party tonight. Your mother has been dead for more than fifty years now. I have never met her. You *do* have seven grandchildren, but they are all scattered, and some are already in college. I think you're confused or perhaps just tired and confusing some facts from the past with the present. I only say this because I love you and I want to help you."

"Help me with what, dear? Did you say something about still being away at college? My sister Joan is still away at college. She must be twenty-one or so now. She's going to be a teacher, you know."

"No!" he screamed. "Great Aunt Joan is not—"

Flo had started her shift about an hour ago and was catching up on treatment rounds that the short-staffed day shift couldn't keep up with. She was changing bandages on ulcerated legs, checking insulin levels on brittle diabetics, and ensuring that IV lines and G-tubes were properly inserted. Fifteen minutes had gone by on Flo's shift when she came upon the sitting room and the sound and very familiar sight of a family member trying desperately to bring his beloved mother or grandmother back to earth from dementia-land. To say that this made the imperious Flo cringe was only a slight understatement.

In her best Caribbean accent, Flo inserted herself into this family dialogue and interrupted Graham mid-sentence. "Reeeally, mon, I think you might remember that Agnes here often sees pictures of Joan—her favorite sister—when she was graduating from that fancy school in upstate New York. Joan is twenty-one. Yes, she is. In that picture of her graduation, she sure is. Isn't she, Miss Agnes? Now you, young man, look just like Tommy, Miss Agnes's brother. Tommy had four children and often met Miss Agnes and your grandfather for Mass and supper on Saturday afternoons. Why, it was their own little family tradition. It's quite a compliment to be thought of as looking like your Great-uncle Tommy, isn't it now, Mr. Graham?"

Graham was rendered utterly speechless and, worse, felt about two feet tall. Again, not knowing where to begin to dig himself out of this heap of embarrassment, he fumbled with, "I can't quite read your name tag. Is it Florence?"

"Uh huh. You can read, can you now?"

"I, I, I am sorry," he stammered. "I mean, I am amazed. I mean, how do you know so much about my family, my grandmother's family? Are you always here on her floor?"

"Well, I guess after twenty years of geriatric nursing you learn a thing or two about working with folks who are in a state of"— Flo whispered to the point of practically mouthing it to Graham— "de-men-tia, or as everyone likes to call it, Alzheimer's. You do know that Alzheimer's is just one form of dementia? It's not its very own nasty disease. It's just a part of the dementia family."

"Why, no, ma'am, I never truly understood that."

"It's Flo, plain and simple. Flo, the evening nurse. So I have a question for you. What did you think happened to your grand-mum?"

"I don't know. I mean, I didn't know. I wasn't sure that I knew or wanted to know what it was or wasn't. I just wanted everything to be the same as when I last saw her a couple of years ago. I didn't know what to expect when I got here today, and then it only got worse as the conversation ensued. I didn't even know . . ." Graham couldn't hold the tears back any longer, "what was real or what wasn't, and then I, I . . . I tried to believe that maybe she was just confused, and that it wasn't all that bad after all. Then, she just started going on about all this crazy shit. I'm sorry, Flo."

"Ain't nothing to be sorry about, my dear. Shit is shit, but what Agnes was saying is most certainly not shit. It just happens to be her reality. The disease does not take away the person, the human being that lives inside her withering body. The dementia only realigns the chain of events of her life. Do you know what I mean? It just messes around with the linear equation of who is where and when it is actually happening. It's almost like—and trust me, I ain't no doctor or research specialist—but I have read enough and lived through this enough that I know it merely takes her brain cells and shovels some off to the side. And then it takes some giant spoon and moves the others around, so when her words travel from her brain to her mouth, the time line of her life is constricted and the oldest—or maybe best—memories are the ones that get to travel down to her mouth. I hope this is making some kind of sense for you, Mr. Graham?"

The entire time Flo was explaining dementia to him in this most beautiful and fascinating method, Graham was both touched by this foreign black woman's generosity of time and spirit and hurt by the realization his precious grandmother was truly suffering from this unforgiving disease. Yet there was a perfect storm of emotions that unleashed the trickle of tears to a full-fledged torrent. Then the realization kicked in that her prison was one of memories. Often they seemed to be warm and fulfilling, focusing on the years that didn't include him or even his mother for that matter. Why? How could he make any sense of this? Didn't she see him in front of her and real- ize who he was, and that she was a grandmother and not a granddaughter? Didn't it jolt her back through this dazed time machine into the present to see that he was the grandson she had known and loved for years? Instead, she was stuck in this past tense of faded, anachronistic memories.

"I never understood or really knew any of this. Thank you, nurse. I mean, Flo."

"That's why I am still here."

Graham left that night and headed over to his favorite watering hole, The Franklin Tap. He ordered a Sam Adams and a shot of Jameson. He took a corner bar seat where he proceeded to brood. Two hours and five beers later, Graham still sat there staring out the window, trying to make sense out of this "fucking dementia thing." Whatever it was, it held hostage his favorite person in life and practically turned her into a stranger. He wondered, *Is she better off dead? I don't know. I just don't know what happened and why I can't seem to do anything about it.*

Rob, the bartender, never particularly cared for hearing his customers talk to themselves, especially after serving the customer about five drinks—always a *problem*.

"Graham, you can't do anything about *what*?"

"My grandma is in a nursing home. I went there for the first time today. And you know what, Pete, she doesn't even know me. Has no idea. Really. She lives in the past, like it's 1957 or somewhere around then. And what has me more pissed off than anything is that I can't do anything about it."

"You can't, really? I think you could at least go up there every day after work and visit with her."

"Thanks for telling me what to do, Pete, because I would never think to—"

"It was a suggestion. And frankly, I don't think you thought of it. Don't run from your troubles or from the realities of living and dying. Or really, the reality of just aging. You know, man, it happens to all of us. I'm just an old bartender, but I can only tell you that she needs you. She may not always recognize you or what year this is, but she is still a person who needs other people to talk to her, to touch her hand, or just to sit with her. That's what you can give her. It's all you've got to give her. And it's what she needs most."

"Thanks. I'm going over now."

"Oh, no, not now, buddy."

Graham could barely contain himself. "What the fuck are you talking about? You told me my grandma needs me and I should go over now to see her. What gives, buddy?"

"You're drunk. It's not the best thing to start doing the right thing tonight. For Christ's sake, buddy, don't think so literally. Start your new, less selfish life tomorrow."

"Good night, man. I think I am all set now. You've showed me, I mean, shown me, the way."

"Good night, Graham. And please take the cab that I called. It's waiting outside the bar right now."

Chapter 16: The Interloper

It was a typical Tuesday, and bingo was the highlight of this otherwise ordinary day. Almost every alert and some-what-alert set of eyes looked up at what they perceived as a blue-eyed god, gliding his way into the activities room. Most couldn't understand why this very handsome man was joining in on their bingo game.

Graham kept looking around for his grandmother but was told she was coming down soon. In the meantime, everywhere he looked, eyes kept following him, sometimes accompanied by a wave, begging him to sit down beside him or her. He started toward an empty seat when an arm reached out and grabbed his hand. Graham was startled at first, but after the second time he placed his other hand on top of the hand that had grabbed his. He looked at who was grabbing him and saw no one he had ever met before, but he did see a human being who must not have experienced any form of human touch in a very long time.

She looked into his deep blue eyes and said, "Thank you, my dear, for coming today. I've been looking for you for so long. Where is your sister? I thought I'd see her too today."

"Oh, ma'am, I think there's a mistake. I am here to see my grandmother, Agnes Nolan. I'm not related to you, but I'm sure I must look like one of your grandsons or nephews or someone along those lines."

"Aren't you sweet, honey? Now if you can just tell me where we are and why we're here. I know that I had to take the garbage out the other day. The snow was starting to fall, and I didn't know what to do next. No one was going to work that day, and then I fell asleep and ended up here. Do you know where my garbage ended up and who's taking care of the house while I recuperate?"

"You know what, ma'am?"

"What, dear?"

"Well, I was *about* to tell you. An old friend of mine once told me this. It seems simple, ma'am, but it's all I know to get through life. It's all good!"

"It's all good. I don't know if I believe in the 'all good' part or the 'it' part or the . . . what are we talking about anyway? I can't think of too much good anymore."

"Do you know Mrs. Nolan? She's my grandma and I was hoping to visit her today. I thought I'd see her here in the day room or the activity room next door."

"Aggie?"

"You know my grandmother? I never knew her nickname was Aggie, but I guess it makes sense."

"I'll tell you if you promise not to abandon me. I kind of liked seeing a handsome young lad chit-chatting with me."

"Well, I think you need glasses, ma'am, but of course I will always check in with you when I come to see my grandma."

"I think she's sitting straight ahead by the nurses' station."

"I think you know a lot about what's going on. Maybe more than when we first met," Graham said with a wink aimed at his newfound friend.

Graham felt a pit in his stomach when he first approached the nurses' station and couldn't find his grandmother. He had always had a little flair for the dramatic, especially when it came to the question of imminent death. He approached the first person behind the desk and asked where Mrs. Nolan was located, as he couldn't find her in any of the usual sitting places.

The woman didn't appear to be a nurse, but she asked Graham how he was related to Mrs. Nolan.

"Grandson." Graham thought, *What is going on? This must not be good. Oh, God. Why did I leave my office and come out to this nurses' station just in time for something like this?*

"Mrs. Nolan was sent to the hospital this morning. She was, ah, *unresponsive* when the unit nurse went in to assist her with morning care. As you must know, she is a full code, so we called 911 immediately and commenced chest compressions right through getting her onto the stretcher and into the ambulance." Seeing his blank stare, she asked, "You are familiar with full code, right?"

"I understand it's a system of making sure the health care provider does everything in their power to ensure that the person dying continues living at all costs to ensure a clear conscience for the relative who made this decision. I absolutely need to talk to my mother at some point very soon about this code directive."

"Well, these decisions are never easy and often done with the individual herself, many years before her faculties have diminished; but I need to speak with you about something else."

After a moment of uncomfortable silence, Graham finally asked, "I can spare you any difficulty here. I'm a grown man. She passed away today, yes?"

"Yes, your grandmother died this morning at the Massachusetts General Hospital. The EMTs and then the doctors and nurses at the hospital did everything they could, but her heart gave out. It was weak and tired. That was 2:43 p.m. today. No matter how old someone is when they die, it's never easy for the loved ones. And, I *am* sorry."

"Please don't be sorry, miss. Here we are, I don't even know your name, and you were just part of the most dreaded moment of my life. Since I was young, I understood she would die, but could never come to grips with what it would be like and how I would take it. But I'm focused on something else: what it felt like for her. Do you know, did she feel the chest compressions and the desperate attempts to breathe life back into her dying body? I mean, well, what do you think?"

"It's Sarah." Small pause. "We never really know what the person is feeling and sensing. They can't talk to us through that third wall. I don't want to sound clichéd, but I want you to believe she probably felt very little pain. I've watched enough deaths here, and I have always followed their eyes. It's like they are already somewhere else, looking at their new surroundings while we think they're still with us only because there is still a bit of a pulse or zigzag on the EKG screen. It gives us this false sense of them still being here, with us."

"Anyway, it's done, and I guess I lived through it. Thanks to you."

"Sir, go home and get some rest."

"I know, but first I just have to ask—did you know her before she wasted away from this disease? Did she ever tell you a coherent story? Did she ever talk to you about her grandkids? Probably not, huh?"

Sarah made the quick decision to forget about the paperwork sitting on her desk. She looked at Graham and knew he needed to allay his guilt and feel better about the fact his grandmother lived and died in a nursing home and she assumed he never bothered to visit until the time of her death.

Sarah told Graham, "I know from her chart that dementia was suspected upon admission in 2007. When Mrs. Nolan arrived, she walked without assistance, ate all her meals in the dining room, had one of the few single rooms, and always dressed impeccably. I know from the past three years that she went downhill quickly. It seemed like one day she was walking down the hall to the dining room like you or I, and the next day she was using a cane. Then I looked again a few days later to find her suddenly in a wheelchair. I don't know why the disease progresses so quickly with some people and not as much in others. Did I hear her talk about her grandchildren? Um, no." The "no" landed like a thud in an empty room.

"I don't really care. I guess I just wanted to understand if she was always as bad as I saw the other day and if she was ever so with-it that she questioned being dumped here."

"Wait a second. No one dumped her here. I remember when her daughter—I assume your mother . . ."

Graham nodded.

"She sat in the admissions director's office crying over not having a choice and begging us to talk her out of admitting your grandmother."

"I guess it's not what I thought." Graham was now teetering on the edge of tears, just as his mother once did according to this story. "I wanted to believe her, and I just couldn't fathom why she couldn't keep Gram at home. Miss, you say 'choice.' What about home care services? Actually, what about my mom quitting her job and staying home with Gram? Yeah, and while I'm at it, what about assisted living?"

"I am more than happy to talk to you some more, but would you like to check in with the rest of your family or even be alone for a bit? The funeral director is also going to need to talk to members of the family to make the arrangements soon. And—"

"You don't want to answer my questions?"

"Sir, um, Graham, if I may. You are grieving. Your mother and her brothers are surely grieving. I just don't think now is the time for a post-mortem on why and how people are admitted to nursing homes."

"If not now, when?"

"Assisted living usually means moving twice."

"What? You'll talk to me?"

Sarah knew she wouldn't want her own son hating her for something that wasn't her fault. She chose health and human services as a profession for a reason. Nothing was going to stop her now from setting this young man straight. "Of course, don't be silly. Assisted living is a great option for an elderly person with unlimited income and a picture of health who doesn't decline sharply. If not, you're prolonging the inevitable. Did your mother have anywhere from seven- to ten-thousand dollars per month for an assisted living apartment?"

"Well, no."

"OK, the other problem not many people know about is limited tolerance for the aging process. Yes, the great and wonderful *assisted living* does not want any elderly people whose aging process includes a fall or even early signs of incontinence. Oh, yeah, and don't look so shocked there, Mr. Person-who-wants-all-the-answers!"

"I just didn't know this."

Sarah continued. "There is no 24-hour nursing staff in assisted living facilities. There are visiting nurse programs which come into the building and maybe a health care director who's a nurse, but not the type of nursing your grandmother came to rely on here. When a person in an assisted living facility falls and has to be sent to the Emergency Room, that resident and his or her family are put on notice that he or she will have to leave and be transferred to a nursing facility. Hence, my original statement, why move twice?"

"Thanks. I think it's time to go see the funeral director," replied a tired Graham.

"Don't you want more answers?"

"Not yet. This is going to have to sink in a bit. Thanks again."

Chapter 17: The Aftermath

Graham, his mother, father, and four sisters convened at the family's homestead. These are the four walls where they were raised until the point of departure for college. As always throughout the family's history, they were immediately drawn to the round kitchen table. A bottle of red wine and a bucket filled with Sam Adams beer were unceremoniously placed on the table. Graham's Uncle Donald joined them about thirty minutes into this impromptu Irish wake.

Donald cried out, "What a shame she didn't just die in her sleep a few years ago rather than end her days in a goddamned nursing home!"

"Donald, stop! That statement is wrong on so many levels!" shouted Graham's mother.

"You wanted your mother to die earlier, to have a shorter life? Just so you could say you weren't responsible for putting your mother in a nursing home? Was it *that* horrible for you, that your mother got to live to the ripe old age of eighty-seven, just because three of those years were in a nursing home? I have to tell you, those nurses were damned good to Mother. I think they did a better job than you, or I, or your investment banker wife could have done."

"Leave Stephanie out of this. This is about you and me and the decisions we made for Mom. And you, Dad—it's about what you chose not to do."

"What the hell does that mean, Donald? My wife of fifty-two years just died. My kids' mother just died. You're going to stand here in judgment of me on the day she died? Why? Because your sister and I both knew we were not equipped to give someone with dementia the level and quality of care they deserved? Is that why? Well, I hate to tell you this, but I hate myself that I didn't know how to care for someone with dementia. But I don't hate myself for having the courage to make a difficult decision to place my beloved wife into the care of people who are trained and certified to deal with people with this disease. Wait, that's a bad choice of wording. They didn't 'deal' with her; they provided care and treated her with respect and dignity. When Mom had 'accidents,' they wiped her butt as if it were nothing. I couldn't do that. Your brother couldn't do that. And I am just guessing that neither you nor Stephanie could do that." As the conversation rose to a crescendo, Fred Nolan, with all composure intact, allowed the tears to fall down his face for the first time that day.

"Dad, Diane, Andy, Graham, I'm sorry, and I don't meant to disrespect this day or Mom's life. It's just that, that, I hated that place and couldn't stand to see her there."

Graham broke in, "But did you do anything about that? Did you take her out and bring Gram to your home? Did you try to man up and look past the aesthetics of the place or, more to the point, pass by your own guilt and do the more selfless thing—go spend time with her there? I did. It hurt like hell to go there at first, but I also had to assuage my guilt. Most importantly, she benefited from the visits. They made her smile."

Donald's sister-in-law, Graham's mother, Diane, was quietly crying and only partially listening to the conversation. She often wondered why her son had not come home for a long time, if only to see the grandmother he was so close to. She was now looking directly at Graham.

"Why? Why are we here, drinking beer and pretending this is some semblance of a normal family? My mother-in-law died today, and we're all a bunch of fucking idiots. We can't even take a minute to celebrate that we *are* together, or more importantly, to possibly state that Mom lived a good, long life. All we can do is fight like idiots over whether her living in a nursing home was a terrible, wretched thing for us to allow to happen or not. Really! What the FUCK is wrong with us? It happens. People who don't know better or feel they have no other recourse but to put people who seem to be demented into nursing homes, so nurses and other professionals can take care of them!"

Graham couldn't hold his shit together another minute. "Ma, who are you calling demented? I think *you're* demented for saying that. Gram wasn't demented or whatever the hell you called her. She was old and had some senility or maybe her arteries had hardened, but are you suddenly on the bandwagon that Grandpa and whoever else made 'the decision' did the right fuckin' thing? I know you want us to sit and talk about what a saint Grandma was and make a few jokes about funny things she said and did along her road, like a true Irish/Scottish wake, but evidently that just isn't going to happen tonight, and if you can't handle that maybe you don't need to hang around."

You could have heard a pin drop. Those sitting around the table looked at their beer, their wine glass, and even their fingernails, but not a soul dared to speak to mother and son. Each was clearly grieving differently. A woman grieves for her own mother like no one else can—for better or for worse. A young man grieves for his father's mother, if she was like a mother, very uniquely. Graham seemed to forget that the woman's husband, sons and daughters-in-law, and daughter were in the room.

"I am not leaving my father's home. And young man, she was your grandmother, not your mother. Don't forget that. You have a mother—she's alive and sitting at this table."

"Then *she* should have acted more like a mother so I wouldn't be here right now grieving for a woman who became my mother. Maybe there were a few Cape Codders or wines you could have left at the bar. And maybe you could have told me the truth about what was happening with Gram's disease. I'll see all of you phonies, who can't open your eyes or talk truth about what's happening in front of our faces, at the funeral home. Good night."

The funeral took place on a cloudy, rainy Thursday morning in March. It was as anyone could expect—light on the old friends, who had died by now, and attended mostly by children, grandchildren, nieces, nephews, and friends of the younger generations. The priest tried to relate to the deceased as if he truly knew her. The songs were standard Catholic funeral fare, and the readings were the usual suspects—the Twenty-third Psalm, John and Paul's funereal verses. As Mass was concluding, the funeral procession followed the pallbearers as they slid her casket onto the wheels of the hearse.

The graveside ceremony was nothing short of depressing. Much like a scene from a movie, no more than twenty-five people stood with black umbrellas in hand, listening to the tired old mutterings of the priest with a background chorus of pelting rain. Graham, his mother, father, grandfather, Uncle Donald, Aunt Stephanie, Aunt Diane, and others watched her casket as it was lowered into the grave, some six feet below the ground the survivors stood upon.

Graham could not enjoy himself at the funeral breakfast— some distant relatives from other states called it a "mercy meal"— nor could he fake it during countless social interactions and conversations meant to take the mourners off task of actually trying to mourn. He finally took a walk past the backyard of his grandfather's house, mostly to clear his head, but more importantly Graham wanted to take stock of his life and ask himself the question: did her life impact mine, and if so, when and how do I make any changes based on these answers?

Chapter 18: A Visitor No More

In some ways it looked like the same place where he had so reluctantly come to visit his grandmother, but the nursing home also looked as he had never seen it before. The walls were not gray, the furniture wasn't as run-down as he had thought, and the atmosphere was not as gloomy as he recalled.

"Hi, I am looking for Carol Jansen. My name's Graham Nolan, and I am starting work here today. I was told to ask for you as you're the volunteer coordinator."

"I am, and the activities director and friend to many a resident. Nice to meet you, and thanks for joining us. How many hours can you give me a month? A week? Or how many hours can you give at all?"

"Well, I, I don't really know yet. I need to make sure I can handle this before estimating how much I can take on."

Carol was taken aback by this. "Handle what? It won't be hard to lend a hand around here. Do you mean it will be hard to be around people who are old and feeble?"

"Oh, gee, no. I'm sorry. I had just started visiting my grandmother here when she passed away."

"Oh, yes, of course. You're Mrs. Nolan's grandson. One of the residents, Millie, told me all about you. She described you to a tee. She had found it odd that Agnes Nolan had a young visitor after a few years of seeing only middle-aged relatives. Millie had wished that she had a young, handsome visitor."

"All right, nice to know, but no need to make me blush."

Carol found herself a little flustered, as she surely did not mean to upset or embarrass her new volunteer. But she also wanted to let him know she knew about his protracted discussion with Sarah, the MDS nurse, the day his grandmother died. She thought she'd leave a little discussion for the home's summer cookout.

"Just forewarning you that these ladies still have eyes, and any gentleman under sixty is going to have to handle a little flirting. But anyway, what did you have in mind?"

"In mind for what?"

Now Carol was truly confused. "For the type of volunteer work you want to do here, silly."

"Oh, yeah, of course. I don't know, didn't realize there was a choice, I guess. I want to help out around here wherever you need help. I can do a few shifts a week. Do you need help on the weekends?"

"I need a friendly visitor."

"A what?"

"Just let me finish explaining. You'll visit people on the weekends while there are no activities scheduled, especially the residents who don't typically receive visitors. Also, Saturdays and Sundays are the biggest days for visitors, which makes the days even harder for the ones who don't have visitors. That's where the friendly visitor concept comes into play."

Graham was quiet for a moment. Just when Carol thought he was going to decline her volunteer idea and possibly get up and leave, he asked, "Carol, did my grandmother have visitors on Saturdays and Sundays?"

"Well, I'm not here every weekend, but I can tell you she had more visitors than many other residents."

"I'm not sure that answer makes me feel much better, but yes, I will be a friendly visitor."

"You'll be a very good one, Mr. Nolan! Allow me to show you around," she said with cheerful sincerity, or was it a level of phoniness? Graham couldn't really tell.

There might be a bit of electricity in the air. Why? Carol was glad she had landed a new volunteer, especially for the staff-challenged weekends. Graham was happy about a chance to redeem himself from his selfishness, though he hadn't realized that yet. He subconsciously knew that if he visited some other elderly folks who needed someone, he could somehow make it up to his Gram for being such a selfish jerk these past few years. Graham had no idea of what a ride he was in for.

Carol began with staff introductions. Graham was formally introduced to the administrator, Sally Cournan and Michael Versey from social services, Flo from nursing and for their second time meeting, he shook hands with Sarah, the MDS nurse. Carol explained Sarah's job had something to do with government reimbursement to the nursing home.

Graham was a little intimidated by all these health care professionals. Despite being a computer programmer, he felt fairly substandard next to all of them. That, of course, was

Graham's problem. And Flo was not the most welcoming when she asked Graham, "What do you know about these people's needs?"

Graham responded, "I don't know, and I'm not sure they communicate their needs well or that others know how to interpret their wishes and needs. I guess my short answer is that I don't know what their needs are. I *am* sure I could guess they need to be loved, and touched, and spoken to with care and compassion."

"Do you really believe this shit you're spouting out, honey?" Flo couldn't help herself, despite being apprised that she was too acerbic by everyone she worked with, especially by her bosses at employee evaluation time.

Not really knowing where to begin or if he should run out the door and avoid this despair-ridden volunteer job, Graham instead just stared at Flo. He could come up with some real smart-ass remarks and espouse the virtues of giving back to the community. He also thought about telling her to go fuck herself and get back to dishing out medications to people who really don't want them anymore.

"Well, *do* you?" she exclaimed.

"I do." Sometimes, Graham surprised himself when some simple truth just shot out of his mouth without a lot of thought. "I think I do anyway. I know I have limited experience, but I have some time on the weekends and a couple of evenings a week. I guess I just wanted to try harder with someone else's grandparents than the performance I put in for my poor old Gram."

"Yes, honey, I know who she was and that she died last week. I know your type too. They're all 'I'm gonna save the world and make a difference for all these poor people with no visitors because I didn't visit my loved one enough.' Well, I know, man—trust me, I know—this do-good shit lasts a week or two."

Graham had dealt with a lot of tough cookies in the internet business and wasn't bothered by Flo's attitude. He decided he had a goal after all, and maybe Flo was putting it in focus better than a Nikon could have. So he continued, "If I give this a try for two weeks, it would be more than I was ever here to see my own grandmother. Yes, I know, shame on me. But wouldn't it be two weeks worth of visits that some of these folks would not have received if I hadn't tried this?" He feared he might be sounding sanctimonious but knew he had to tell it like it is. "If I were supported in this effort, maybe my tenure would have a better prognosis." Yeah, throw in a good medical term, Graham thought. "I'd have some great first impressions about how to go about this and some encouragement or even some direction. But you know, Flo, now I'm a little more determined to do this and see what they're really all about and how I can do something to break through their imprisoned faces, and somehow touch them. Thanks."

"You're welcome."

That was it. No grand gestures or apology or more devil's advocate arguments, just a simple "You're welcome." Graham was kind of lost and simply replied, "That's it?"

"Just making sure you have a clue and know what you're getting into."

"Got it." Graham looked for Carol, but she was gone—gone for *how much* of the dialogue was unclear, but here he was, alone with this salty old nurse who was determined to teach him a thing or two. "Hey, Flo, where do I go from here?"

"Take a walk to the end of this corridor, and you *will* find a sun room—we call it a day room—and you'll see three or four of our residents sitting in geriatric recliners. We call those 'geri chairs.' They don't get too many visitors. They'll probably sit there for a few hours until dinner is served at five o'clock. Sit with them. That's all."

"Thanks, Flo. I will. But is that all? Just sit there?" Graham was excited and nervous at the same time with this first directive.

"Yep. You'll see."

What he'd see he didn't know, but he left her medication cart area and hurried off to his first mission. He had no idea where his "boss" had gone and whether she would sanction this assignment, but something told him to listen to this old black nurse. So off he went down this corridor to a new world. As he walked, his head quickly turned to the left, then to the right as he passed each bedroom. Many people were just lying in their beds, some were watching television, and others were simply sleeping, while some people seemed to be writhing in discomfort. One woman yelled out, "Will you help me?"

Graham took a deep breath as he considered whether to follow Flo's directions to a tee, stop and see what the woman needed, or better yet, run back to Flo and tell her about this screaming woman. He made an about face, running for Flo.

"Flo, there's a woman about three quarters down the hall who seems to be screaming out in pain. I didn't know what to do and thought you needed to do something or—"

"306 or 308?"

"Huh?"

"Honey, what room was she in?"

"The one with the wheelchair at the end of the bed."

"Oh, thanks so much for narrowing that down for me!" Flo sarcastically exclaimed.

"Please, just help her."

"Lead the way." When they reached room 308, Flo looked at him and said, "That's Evelyn. She has no idea where she is or what time it is. She doesn't know why she screams. The doctors have not been able to determine if there is any real pain. If I had to rely on my old Haitian father's voodoo teachings, I'd say she is stuck between two worlds and that is causing her serious mental anguish. She is either trying to die or something on the other side is starting to pull her. Just stand in the doorway, honey."

"Evelyn. Evelyn, this is Flo, your nurse. Listen to me." Nothing. "Evelyn, I am going to turn on your radio." Flo turned on her radio, which was already tuned to an easy-listening station and set to a relatively low volume. She then pulled up the bedside chair, sat down, and took hold of

Evelyn's hand. She held it, stroked it, and told her everything would be all right.

The screaming stopped. Graham was paralyzed with wonderment while standing at the doorway. He just stared at Flo, then at Evelyn, and at their two hands. He wondered if Flo or another nurse had held his grandmother's hand. He wondered if he could do that for a stranger. He would soon find out.

"Come here, boy. Sit right on this chair." Graham entered the room, followed the latest orders, took Flo's seat, and waited. Flo continued, "Take her hand."

Graham slowly reached for Evelyn Larsen's hand, and his world as he knew it melted away and became something new. Something exciting and full of promise.

Her screaming was supplanted with a purr-like sound. She even opened her eyes. They were a milky pale blue that bordered on gray. She looked at Graham and smiled.

For a small moment in time, Graham looked into her eyes and realized he should continue the petting of her hand that Flo had started and encouraged. When Evelyn seemed to gaze right into Graham's eyes, the first tear streamed down his face. He knew he was in for the ride of a lifetime.

Flo excused herself and said she would call Katie or Carol to let them know of his whereabouts. Graham thanked her and continued with his new connection, his new friend, his new surrogate.

"So, your name is Evelyn Larsen. Mine's Graham Nolan. I just started working here. I mean, working at your home. Can you hear me?"

Evelyn didn't wear a hearing aid, and may have had quite good hearing, but whether her mind could process his sentences and questions was unclear. Graham didn't exactly understand this yet; instead, he looked intently at Evelyn and asked again whether she could hear him.

As time slipped past him and he continued holding Evelyn's hand, she lay there looking at him as if to say, "Yes, I do" and "Where have you been all my life?" Evelyn's wrinkled, dry lips slowly parted into a crooked smile.

Assuming this was a sign Evelyn could hear, Graham asked, "What can I do for you? Can I get you anything? Please, just let me know."

When this yielded nothing more than the smile that was now a fading smile, Graham began to understand that perhaps she could not hear after all, and the smile was merely a reaction to his kindness. Feeling paralyzed by the moment again, Graham decided to remain with her. He sat and held Evelyn's hand. The clock ticked on.

Graham finally made it back to the corridor and took the right toward the end to find his first assignment. He found them. It seemed to be a safe assumption anyway, that these people were his assignment. There they were, lying in a row in their reclining geriatric chairs. Lying, not sitting. There was not an aide, nurse, or attendant of any sort to be found. Graham thought to himself, *What if I didn't happen to volunteer, who would have seen these three ladies lying here?*

One lady, who he learned was named Joan, was hitting the side of her mouth with a spoon—repeatedly. She would place the spoon back in her dish, try to scoop up more of the pureed food that looked like mush, and attempt to get it to her mouth. This attempt repeatedly failed, and the food eventually landed on the floor, her tray, and the side of her face and neck. Graham thought it really was nothing short of neglect that this woman was left her to feed herself when she clearly could no longer do so. He asked Joan if he could help her with the food, but received a blank stare in return.

Next to Joan was a woman named Verna. Verna was quite talkative and wanted to know a good deal of information about Graham, who he was and what he was doing there. When he asked Verna her name, she wasn't too clear. Graham also asked how long she had lived here. That answer was also dubious. Graham really didn't know what to do at this point. He had no real directions or training and didn't know if he was qualified or allowed to feed them. But it did not sit well that there were no nursing home staff assisting the woman whose hand-eye coordination no longer served her.

Graham approached the third lady and looked for the name card on her meal tray, but it stated only her food allergies and seemed to be missing the owner of the allergies. Her plate was untouched, and the food was dried out and appeared cold. Graham felt a lump in his throat growing and couldn't get past the thought that these ladies were forced to live this way. The image of his grandmother lying in one of these geri chairs by herself, with no staff nearby, remained in his mind's eye. *Did she live like this? I didn't see this the day I came to visit, but who knows*, he thought to himself. He made a decision right there, at that moment. He was staying with this volunteer job. He was coming back tomorrow.

"Let me take your napkin and help you, Joan." He continued trying to be all things to all people in this forgotten day room. "Verna, tell me more about yourself. Miss, uh—I can't read your name on your wrist band—would you like any of this food or do you prefer it heated up?" There was no reply.

"All right, let's see what's here that isn't too cold. How about this applesauce? Do you want to try it?"

"She don't eat that. She waits and tries a little of the meat and vegetables later on." Graham spun around, quite startled to see a CNA had joined them in this day room.

"Were you assigned to these women for meal assistance?"

"Who the hell are you to ask me that?"

"I'm a volunteer here, and I know a thing or two about elderly folks choking on their food if they are neglected while eating. She could have died, and this nursing home could have gotten sued."

With quite a huff and click of her heels, she turned and said, "I'm telling my supervisor about you and what you said, you busybody!"

The next day Graham came back for more. The first day not only didn't scare him away, but also it emboldened him to get back there and make a difference any way he possibly could.

"Where can I start today?" Graham asked as soon as he saw his boss.

"What brought you back?" she asked.

"What made you think I wouldn't come back?" he quickly retorted.

"They usually get scared away."

"That's it? *Your* volunteers get *scared* away?"

"Well, yeah, they sure do," she said firmly. "Why?"

"I thought you paid attention yesterday? That's what you indicated so clearly to me. Regardless, I want to do this and thought you would be a little more encouraging."

"I'm sorry. And please don't think I am not desperate for volunteers, but I know this is not easy work, and it doesn't work out for everyone. A lot of volunteers have thought there would be a lot of hand-holding with sweet little old ladies who are sitting around knitting. I think you might have seen this doesn't match that fantasy."

"No, it doesn't, but I'm still in. Where do I go today?"

Chapter 19: Decisions Challenged

Graham did go back, day after day he did, giving a few extra hours on the weekends. In fact, he *couldn't* stay away. It was like watching a train wreck or chasing an ambulance. He wasn't sure why, but he knew the place needed him, or possibly he needed the place. He soon learned all the protocols, schedules, and most importantly, who was who. He learned that the director of nursing was *in charge*. The administrator thought he was, but he wasn't from what Graham observed. He also soon learned that the director of rehab rates high because she brings in the cash for "the building." Social services helped the business office with bringing in the cash by gathering and submitting all the bank statements and other forms to get the residents on Medicaid. Graham also learned that his boss, the director of recreation therapy, was at the bottom of the food chain at the nursing home. He realized that "the building" was how the business-minded folks referred to the residents' home. *Hmm*, he thought.

As the weeks passed, Graham figured out who simply went through the motions versus staff who seemed to be there because they truly cared for the elderly and disabled individuals in their care. He saw more than he cared to see or had bargained for. Also, families started showing an interest in him and even asked him to keep an eye on their loved one while he was on and they weren't around. One weekend afternoon, he bumped into a visitor.

"Are you new here?" asked the man who was wheeling his mother into the elevator.

"Sort of. I'm a volunteer, been here a couple of months. I've been helping out after work and on weekends since shortly after my grandmother died. I don't think I've seen you here. Is your father or mother here?"

"Joan Hamilton is my mom. You may have met her," Luke told him.

"I'm Graham Nolan," he said as he stuck out his hand for a handshake.

"I'm Luke Hamilton. They shook hands and got into the elevator. Graham still hadn't figured out how best to phrase things to staff or family, so he stumbled a little as he asked his next question.

"Why did your mother end up here?"

"What gives you the right to ask me about something so personal? Hey, I thought you were just a volunteer?"

Graham stood stunned and ready to spit out a quick apology when Luke spoke again.

"I'm sorry, I shouldn't have snapped at you like that. It's just that I, well, I still . . ."

"Still what?" Graham asked.

"I still haven't answered that question for myself."

"No, I'm sorry, Mr. Hamilton. I guess it isn't the kind of question one asks a stranger a minute after meeting."

"Buddy, it's Luke. And really, it's no big deal. We have that in common. How did your grandmother end up here?" After they exited the elevator, they walked toward the front lobby and continued talking.

"I'm actually *still* trying to answer that question. I was away at school when it happened. It's easy to blame my mother for doing this to my Gram, her own mother—I was really fuming mad at her at first. Shortly after I arrived home, she died. Then I was too numb to focus on it, but it still gnaws at me, trying to figure out why she did that to my Gram. There wasn't even a phone call to me out in California. I could have—"

Luke interrupted, "You could have *what*? Left school and rushed back to help your mother change your grandmother's diapers? I know you mean it sincerely and probably had the best intentions, but think about it."

"I have. That's why I come here after work to volunteer. I want to meet her again and assuage my guilt for having spent so many years away from her. It was for the last three years of her life—the years that happened to end right here."

"I think that's why I visit my mother as much as I do. She doesn't know me anymore. The Alzheimer's has taken over."

"Yeah, I see that disease in a lot of the folks around here."

"Well, that's when I feel less alone, less guilty, actually. I see she's not alone in this nightmare, and I see other sons and daughters, and grandsons and granddaughters coming in when they can, because they probably went through the same thing I did." Luke paused, looked Graham right in the eye, and said, "Man, I've taken enough of your time. Thanks for asking me the question. I'll see you around."

"Sure, nice to meet you, Luke. Glad the question wasn't so bad after all."

"Well, if only coming up with the answer wasn't so bad either. Let's work on that one."

Graham walked back in and headed to the elevator. This time, Flo was getting on.

"Young Mr. Nolan, how do you like being part of St. Matthew's?"

"I'm learning more every day, many thanks to you, Flo. Actually, I like coming here a lot more than my day job. In fact, I am spending more hours here than I spend at my day job."

"So, you still looking for answers to your questions?"

"I am. Yes, ma'am, *I am*. I'll see you later, Flo. Thanks again."

That same weekend, Graham stopped over to his parents' house for dinner. Things had settled down there since his grandmother's death, and everyone went back to their routines once the funeral was over and the casserole dishes were all returned to their rightful owners. After dinner, Graham sat in the backyard on his mother's chaise lounge chair. A few moments later, his father came out with a cup of tea and a sweatshirt.

"Graham, thought you might need this."

"Thanks, Dad. Um, you know I love you, right?"

"Wow, where did that come from?" Dad was both taken aback and saddened. His biggest fear was that the other shoe was about to drop. He loved his son more than anything, but these words were never exchanged easily, and this could mean something was up, as in, "I love you, but . . ."

"Don't know, but may have something to do with my volunteer work."

"Volunteer work? Didn't know you were volunteering somewhere. Where?"

"St. Matthew's."

You could have knocked him over with a feather. He stopped and stared at Graham and finally muttered, "Why would you do that to yourself? It's been hard enough for all of us, hasn't it? You were especially hard on your mother and me for putting your Gram in the nursing home, remember?"

"I know, Dad, but this is unlike anything I've ever experienced. I probably started this out of guilt, but I can honestly tell you I am drawn to it now. I want to, no actually, *need to* be there. I barely want to go to the office anymore. I just want to get there and help in any way I can."

"Hey, I think it's great you're giving back to the community and doing something that most people wouldn't do. By the way, what is it you *do* there?"

"Anything they need me to do that doesn't require a certificate or license. I do transport sometimes. That means pushing the residents in their wheelchairs from one part of the facility to another. I've also been taught to help feed people who aren't a choking risk. Best part of all is helping the activities department with activities. It's great fun, really!"

"I've never seen you quite like this. No, really, well—maybe when you got your first car. Keep doing what you're doing, son. And I am pretty sure you know that I love you too."

During dinner, Graham went through a similar dialogue with his mother. She didn't come around quite as quickly as her husband but was supportive, yet quite inquisitive, not quite in a disapproving manner. They both promised to stop by and see some of Graham's "clients," the former neighbors of the family's "Gram."

Graham left and headed back to his favorite neighborhood bar. Tonight was different from that night not long ago when he came here to drown his sorrows. While he slowly sipped his Harpoon IPA, Graham thought about how he could change his life. Perhaps he could make it a lot less self-centered, although he did wonder what was wrong with focusing on himself and doing the right thing for others by making himself into someone who can make a difference.

He told his bartender he was volunteering at a nursing home now. After an obligatory, "That's nice," there was silence. The bartender clearly didn't understand why a talented computer programmer making lots of money, or so he assumed, would want to spend his precious off hours working in a smelly old nursing home.

"What's the matter, Rob, you've never spent time at a nursing home?"

"Graham, I've spent too much time in them. Three of my four grandparents ended up in nursing homes—two at your St. Matthew's. Not only am I making sure that neither of my parents end up in one, I am determined never to step foot in one again. They stink."

"Geez, you have no idea how hard the nurses and aides work, not to mention all the kitchen workers and laundry and housekeeping staff. They never stop from the minute they get in until their shift is up. I don't think anyone knows what they go through."

"Shit! On a busy Friday night, I'm running from one end of this bar to another. I know all about not stopping over the course of my shift. But what are they really getting done? My grandfather was always sitting in his own piss—I mean *urine*—when I went to see him."

"I wonder how many patients his CNA was assigned to that day?"

"Graham, hmmm? Are you trying to defend them?"

"No, Rob, nursing homes are not where we *choose* to send our parents and grandparents, but they are not all bad. I am just starting to learn a little bit more about the people there."

Graham continued volunteering at St. Matthew's over the next few months. Saturday-only was soon Sunday volunteering too, and Wednesday nights were added before long. Graham found himself missing the place when he wasn't there.

His father continued to doubt his motives and whether it was the best use of his spare time. Even Rob, the bartender, found it odd that his favorite customer was spending so much time at a place that stank of urine and could just as well be shut down for all Rob cared. It almost became a challenge that as more people questioned Graham about his volunteer work, he became all the more determined to adhere to his schedule there and do what he could for these people who seemed forgotten by time, family, and society.

When Graham was at St. Matthew's, something in him came alive. It was ironic considering he often had a lump in his throat when he walked the halls toward his next task. Graham wanted to be there to satisfy an urge to do something for these poor elderly people who seemed to have so little left in their lives, but he also needed to be there to deal with his guilt over abandoning his grandmother so he could live halfway around the world attaining more graduate degrees.

Graham envied Michael and Sally from social services. They seemed to be the saviors of St. Matthew's residents. CNAs and nurses were the culprits when there were accusations of bad care. The CNAs were the staff that families could easily point fingers at when someone appeared to be neglected, but it was Sally and Michael who were forever smoothing things over with families and solving their real or perceived problems. Graham once saw Michael with two residents, helping them through to the point of reconciliation. One had accused the other of coming into her room and stealing things from her bureau drawers. They were practically in tears when he started the process and were laughing and smiling when he was done. Michael wheeled them both—one chair in each hand—back to the day room, where they promptly forgot what had just transpired. Success!

Another day, as Graham was passing the social services office, he saw Sally talking to a family member, a daughter perhaps. The daughter was adamant that her mother was being abused. Sally was letting her know this was a distinct possibility and she would surely investigate. At the same time, Sally also communicated there was a good chance nothing may have happened, as the elderly easily bruise and have skin tares from just about any contact.

Graham was overwhelmed with all the issues—real or perceived—that were inherent in operating a nursing home. A few months before, Graham had been sure that if he were back in Boston when his grandmother went downhill, he would have helped his mom divert Gram from coming to St. Matthew's. But the more time he spent there, the more he was conflicted; all he could think of was whether there was a better way to do this. Sally and Michael sure seemed to know how things should be and how families should be communicated with and treated. They also seemed to take the time to talk to—not at—the residents and ensure that they were treated with respect and dignity. They each had a soothing way about them. Graham clearly hoped that his Gram had spent time with Sally or Michael. He wanted to be more like them, too.

Chapter 20: Loneliness Speaks

There they were in the courtyard. Another winter passed, as did a few of the residents. Millie was dead now. Frannie died at the beginning of winter. John took to his bed and died a few days later from pneumonia. George's heart finally gave out one day. And Agnes Nolan was found unresponsive a couple of months back. But there were still some of the group who came here last fall to sit and stare or argue with one another about who stole whose belongings from nightstands.

Joan and Olivia were both still there. Verna sat in one of the few chairs not on wheels. Rita joined Cecelia and Connie in a separate semi-circle. Doris was wheeled out along with Charlotte and Bertha, who was now a wheelchair user too. She was completely catatonic, but still somehow able to be transferred to a chair. There were a few new residents who were now joining the courtyard crew—Mary Taylor, Tom Perrota, and Rose Freitland.

And there they sat. Graham Nolan came out to deliver snacks and try and engage the group in some form of meaningful dialogue. This was his goal.

Joan said, "Where did it go? The calendar says 2008. Wasn't it just 2007?" Silence then ensued throughout the courtyard. "Olivia, are you there? Can you hear me? I have been trying to get through to you for years, and you're still not listening."

Olivia replied, "Where did what go, you old battle axe?"

Joan retorted, "You're not funny, and I'm no older than you. In fact, I am more than a year younger." More silence, more looking at each other, somewhat crossly this time. "Where did *what* go?"

"The year. Many of the people that lived here. Our homes, but our lives, mostly. I don't know. I just don't know, dear. It's spring again, and we're being pushed out here again. Oh, I suppose the fresh air is nice, but what's the point, really?"

"What's the point, Joan? Really, I have never. I have to ask, are you happy with our little circle of life here? This is all we've got. Three meals a day, a little single bed stuffed in a tiny room with a near perfect stranger, a few games of bingo a week, and sitting around in a circle on this slab of concrete a couple of times a week every May through September. That's the point."

"Olivia, I don't even notice anymore."

"Well, I want you to. I need someone else who's still 'with-it' to care. I need someone to help me *do something* about it. Well, I suppose at least to listen to me complain about it."

"I do. I really do, dear. In fact, I've noticed that it seems every time we gather again out here, there are a few new faces added and a few old faces missing. I know as well as you that if they're not up in their bed, slowly dying, then they've already died. And you know what scares me?"

"What, Joan?"

"That we won't even be remembered. I don't even mean by our families who dumped us here, but by each other. You know, we are all we've got for family now. Each other, that is. And we're lucky if the nurses or Sally or Michael even bother to tell us someone died. I never knew that George died, did you?"

"Nope."

"Frannie had the big Catholic Mass in the chapel, so that was a little different. But typically, it's just another day when one of them has left us. I'm scared, Olivia!"

"Let's face it, Joanie, when we live to be this old and suffer through all the indignities of aging, we've outlived most or all of our friends and original family. That leaves the children, grandchildren, and great-grandchildren who don't give a damn to bother about us to come around and th—"

"And then come to the wake and funeral and all the wailing that goes with it as if they lost a close friend."

"*Well*, I wasn't going to phrase it quite like that, but yes, our families will show up for us."

"Some of them anyway, Olivia! I'm scared. There's nothing after this. It really is our last stop. Sort of like a way station," Joan said.

"I don't know about 'scared,' I just don't want to be forgotten."

"Who does?"

While iced tea was being served, those familiar sounds and phrases started once again and disturbed what little peace others were enjoying or at least trying to enjoy.

"I want to go home. Someone help me get out of here! I just need to get home." These chants got louder and more repetitive.

These mantras continued with no more or no less pain emanating from Connie's mouth, still not knowing where she was or who she was. She simply knew that she wasn't at the place she referred to as home.

Graham had stepped into this scene and took it all in as he continued going about the task at hand. He had learned that no one in the courtyard was connected to each other prior to being placed, but they had subsequently been thrown together in this group living arrangement and, whether they liked it or not, they hung out with the same people. Yet they were different when it came to varying levels of cognition, likes, dislikes, and backgrounds. Graham could clearly see that Joan and Olivia were impaired physically and using wheelchairs, but from their conversation they presented well—and well above Connie and Doris when it came to coherence and effectively living in this world. At these times, he had learned to divert Connie's behavior of shouting out her mantra. He also tried to engage her in discussions with Rose, the new admission. He soon learned from conversations with her son that Rose's son held out as long as possible at home before feeling forced to place Rose at St. Matthew's. It seemed to be a pattern he took comfort in.

Rose was forgetting who she spoke with earlier in the day. Asked what she was doing that evening, she would always reply, "Nothing that I know of." When she began forgetting everything that was discussed with her as recently as five minutes ago, her husband and son made the decision to send her to St. Matthew's Nursing Care Center. That's the official name that they were told was the licensed facility to trust her life with.

Rose seemed to think she knew Connie from a previous life arrangement and kept smiling and waving at her like a long lost neighbor or friend. Connie yelled to Rose at one point, "Who do you think you are to look at me like that? I won't be looked at that way!" Olivia screamed mild obscenities at Charlotte, and Bertha then yelled something similar at Doris, who can't yell at all.

Graham stood in the middle of the courtyard and sternly yet lovingly called out, "Let's not do this anymore. Let's live for today and not worry about tomorrow. Then we can stop feeling angry and lashing out against each other." It was a wee bit dramatic, but nonetheless there was silence for a few moments. Graham went from chair to chair and touched each person's shoulder or arm and reassured them he was there for them. They responded with a mix of smiles, consternation, and non-expressions, but a calm prevailed for a few minutes until the next outbreak.

Joan couldn't stop thinking about the episode. It sometimes got to her that she was one of the sanest people there. There were times when she was as proud of this fact as if it were a badge of honor. Today, it was a mix of wishing she didn't have the faculties to understand what had just happened and realizing she was living in a circus with other eighty-something-year-olds who were acting like kids fighting over a ball on a pre-school playground.

Joan also couldn't stop thinking about why she was here. She assumed that since she was in a wheelchair and her bedroom at home was on the second floor, there was no choice for her daughter but to place her here. As Joan drifted off trying to remember the events of two years ago that led to her coming here to live, she couldn't wrap her mind around what the precipitating event might have been, or even the day before they drove her to St. Matthew's. *Did I pack clothes?* she wondered. *Did they trick me or did they actually tell me they were sending me to live in a nursing home, and I merely went along with it—without a fuss?*

Joan finished her thoughts with a real turn—wishing God would take her. All these thoughts were spinning in her head so fast, and she truly just wanted to die rather than go on living in this insane asylum. If it weren't for the friendship she had forged with Olivia, Joan would have tried to figure out a way to get back home. But since they were in the same boat, and both knew that their respective son and daughter had sold their respective homes, they had a commonality that bonded them and kept them sane. Sort of.

"What are you thinking about, Joan?"

"Oh, Graham, I forgot you were still out here. Not much. Just thought it was tough for Connie and Doris and some of the others to still be dragged out here. It just doesn't seem to suit them anymore. Don't you think?"

"Well, I'm just a volunteer, and I could ask the nurse or Sally or Michael in social services, but it does seem as if the fresh air has got to be good for them. Wouldn't you agree?"

"It's not that it wouldn't be good for them, it's more about whether they even know anymore where they are and what they are doing. Leaving the television room for this court-yard is another unwelcome invasion in their otherwise tidy routine."

"Are you telling me that if your mental health declines, you want to just stay in your room breathing the same air every day and never allowing the staff to take you outside? Does it also mean you wouldn't even want to miss a bingo game in the middle of the winter just because it is a part of a routine?"

Joan started to cry. Graham moved close and held her hand. This made her cry more. Graham apologized and asked, "Did that offend you, Joan?"

"No, I am glad you phrased it like that."

"I meant the touching your hand part."

"No, I haven't been touched in years other than the poking and prodding for blood pressure readings and the like. But to answer your question, no, I will not want to be carted around when it gets to the point that I have no idea who I am."

"But you will still have physical needs. A need for fresh air and movement."

"I will just want to die when that happens."

"Joan, don't say that."

"Why? It's what I think about the others. I sit here and hope for their sake that they will go some night in their sleep and not have to continue suffering through these indignities."

"But they're alive. They still have life in them. They breathe, and their blood pumps through their body."

"I am sorry if I am offending some Christian sensibility, but I have to tell you, dear, that this is not living. That's not how they wanted to be living, and it is certainly not how I want to live. Olivia and I have a pact to kill the other when that happens to our minds."

"You didn't tell me that. You can't do—"

Joan interrupted. "Yes, I can, and I did, and you won't stop us, young man."

Graham went home that night wondering what kind of volunteer job he had gotten himself into and what he would do with this information pertaining to assisted suicide in his midst. He thought about his grandmother and what her final months and days were like. How much did she know about her life and surroundings? Did she realize she had dementia through some sudden glimpses through dementia's shadows? Or did his Gram ever want to kill herself or have some death pact with a friend? Did she wish death upon herself? Or can a person with dementia even know enough to have these thoughts? He wondered constantly about this—at what point do you still know enough to know you are going down that road, down a dusky tunnel that keeps getting darker? When is the point in the tunnel that the lights are about to go out and you say no, I am not going one more step in this tunnel? Then you find out you can't step backward, so you freeze yourself in one position. So could this be the point— if one exists—where you can't step back and choose not to step forward? So an egg timer goes off, warning that you have two minutes to figure a way out, whether it is to find the nearest razor blade or purposely bang your head in the tub to drown a terrible but merciful death?

One thing for sure was that Graham was going to talk to his parents and sister about doing living wills immediately. He had already begun writing his own. The catch was that there didn't seem to be a provision for taking one off life support for early or middle stage dementia. Even Dr. Kevorkian wouldn't assist with a suicide of someone who wasn't in the end stage of the disease.

Graham thought about all his new found friends at St. Matthew's, and who once thought about suicide and who might be thinking these thoughts today. But worse, he thought of who was trapped in a body/mind combination that allowed glimpses of reality. Then he wondered what they did with that momentary flash of light. Do they reach out for help or do they yell, "Get me out of here?" Wait. Graham *had* heard those cries for help. *Is there a connection here?* he wondered.

Might that be what Connie means when she incessantly cries out her mantra of going home? Does she have momentary glimpses of reality that manifest in cries for an escape?

Has any university's gerontology program ever even studied this? Once you've fallen down the rabbit hole of dementia, does the mind have the opportunity to slide past the plaque that blocks the mind from reality and see some light, however cloudy? Graham couldn't stop himself from wondering who was behind these masks and what their prison was like. He could see the outward effects of the prison—the indignities of defecating and urinating on oneself without even realizing it, being fed by someone because you don't know what to do with a fork, and being told to quiet down like a child at 7:30 at night because everyone else was in bed already.

Graham decided this night that he was going to understand this disease and its effects better by interviewing the residents. He realized it might be futile, yet he knew there would be some way to elicit even vague responses from them. As the night progressed, Graham pondered the questions he would ask. The key was, if there was only enough time or enough lucidity for one question, what would it be? Was "How did you land here?" too basic? Yes. Graham wanted to know so much more, such as, "What was your former life like? What do you think about each day? Are you afraid of dying? What do you think of your family? Do you think they could have kept you at home? How often do they visit?"

He wanted to ask every question. He would simply ask Flo for her advice about which ones and how many. As he continued with the mental gymnastics, he countered his last thought with the most logical answer. "I cannot predict this." Graham thought aloud, "These poor people have dementia. It will be what it will be, and I might get one answer per interview or I might get seven, but I know that I will at least ask, 'How did you end up here?'"

Graham knew he was more than a little obsessed with knowing how elders end up living in nursing homes. He was driven by his personal agenda considering his surprise upon moving home after a few years in California. All these months later and he still wanted to reconcile his mother's decision to "place" his precious Gram into a nursing home. He wanted to know what Gram's wishes were compared to how she ended up spending her final couple of years. Time to figure this out, Graham thought. *Game on—let the surveys begin!*

Graham knew every resident of St. Matthew's had a story to tell, despite the limitations dementia might have imposed on them. He was determined to listen to their stories and to give each of them a safe outlet for unloading their pain. Graham also had theories about what they really knew and felt, despite his or her ability to articulate or to convince a clear-minded individual that they weren't totally "gone."

Chapter 21: Where Do
We Go From Here?

Graham was looking at his watch while people-watching the eclectic groups of folks meandering into the Starbucks on Tremont Street. They were like beads on a necklace, the kind you'd find in an artsy seaside colony. Tremont was in a trendy neighborhood, yet with a juxtaposition of run-down Puerto Rican projects adjacent to the million-dollar duplex condominiums.

How Sally Cournan lived in one of these condos was gnawing at Graham. He had lived in a small studio in Berkeley to afford his Bay City existence. He figured her husband must have a good job that allowed Sally the luxury of doing something she enjoyed for little pay. She was a bit of an enigma to him. How could someone really like coming to work every day as much as Sally did? He theorized that she disliked her home-life, and work was a welcome respite from whatever that entailed. A social worker should keep their energy to be prepared for the next death, the next complaint, the next sobbing family, but to also always be smiling and never complain. This chick just wasn't real. Graham was determined to ask her if it was all true. Was she really that intrinsically good? Graham had heard from many a staff member how Sally took the time to counsel staff too. She listened to their family problems, money problems, heard about boyfriends who abused them, and parents who had beaten them many years ago. She talked to nurses about quitting smoking and kitchen staff about how to live a healthier life without alcohol.

Sally never judged. She was an incredibly good "active listener." Graham had learned that term in college at some point and never paid much attention to it, but now it suddenly gained meaning with the embodiment of the term before his eyes. He was done researching, he thought, and ready to make a decision about graduate school and what might be at the center of his thesis. He wanted to talk to Sally about Social Work versus Health Care Administration. He also wondered what Sally would think about him getting a doctorate in gerontology. It is a lost population. Nothing too sexy about studying the elderly with their sagging skin, slowly losing all their charms—is there? So everyone studies pediatrics, cancer, and AIDS, but not much about the art of aging. Graham almost didn't care about any money after the past year of being among some of the most vulnerable and sad souls. He could always figure out his finances. No rocket science there, just live within his means, he always told himself. Graham was by no means perfect, but he was usually driven by pragmatism and good old common sense.

"Oh, Graham, I am so sorry. I must be at least fifteen minutes late, and to make matters worse, I live three blocks from here. The baby——"

Graham cut her off. "Sally, I just sat down with my coffee. Hey, you're doing me a favor. It's Sunday anyway. Who keeps track of time on Sundays?"

"Oh, you are *so* sweet. I'm not doing you a favor. I love talking about what we do."

"We? I don't do what you do. I'm just a lowly volunteer stumbling my way through a maze of new life lessons. You're the pro. A real professional."

"No, really, stop with the compliments."

"Wow. Completely modest to top it off. I mean it, you're a pro. I will admit, I have watched you, studied you almost like a painting. I have never seen anyone with so much empathy and, not meaning to be corny, but it looks like love. Not sure if it's love for the job or for the people."

"OK, let's start there. It certainly isn't for St. Matthew's. I love the residents. They're the reason I come to work every day."

"I figured," Graham said, "but how did you get so good at it? And I've been wondering, did something happen to your own grandparents? You're very at home with their needs and this whole nursing facility setting. In fact, you seem to be in tune with who they are as people and still see them as human beings who need love and attention."

"Do you mind if I just run up to the counter to grab a coffee?"

"Please."

Sally added first, "' Home,' not facility, and 'parent,' not grandparent."

"Oh, my God, I am so sorry to hear that."

"Coffee first, remember?"

Sally settled in with her mocha coffee creation. "So, you are sorry to hear that my parents lived in a nursing home. Why?"

"Well, they must have been young, and you just seem too, um, knowledgeable about services and alternatives so that this type of thing shouldn't have happened to them. You know what I mean?"

"So, are you saying someone like me should have known better? Better than sending their parents up the river to a dreaded nursing facility or 'institutionalized,' as some people call it?"

"No, Sally, I, geez, I can't tell you how sorry I am. I didn't mean to say anything like that. I am still trying to figure this all out. You have to remember, I came back from California to find out my grandmother was living in a nursing home for over a year. I barely got used to it, well, actually I didn't get used to it, but anyway, she was suddenly dead. I think that even she was too young to have been placed in a facility, that's why I was surprised your parents were both in one."

"Relax, dude. No, really, take it easy. You clearly don't know me." Sally took a breath and enjoyed a few sips of her coffee while Graham sat in stunned silence. "My mother had multiple sclerosis and was using a wheelchair. Her arms

and legs had become so atrophied they were effectively useless. And, I don't care if that word's not politically correct.
My father, who is about 150 pounds soaking wet, tried to
get her in and out of the tub and couldn't. I went in to help
him once, and she screamed for me to leave. She said no
seventeen-year-old daughter of hers would have to see her
mother's naked, crippled body like that. We tried to calm her
down with the usual platitudes and tell her I was a woman
too, but she wouldn't stop screaming until I left the bathroom. My father strained his back pretty badly that day and
had to miss the next few weeks from his job as a truck driver.
My mom was a secretary and had given that up a year or so
prior to this event. It wasn't easy. My father actually started
seeing a therapist arranged through the EAP at his company.
You know the big supermarket chain with the yellow and
purple logo? She, the therapist that is, saved his life, he always said. She helped him realize he wasn't doing my mom
any favors living like this. She would go hungry sometimes
during the day when my brother and I were at school and he
was driving. He figured that out, we hadn't. She knew—the
counselor, that is—about some nursing homes and told him
about the one that specialized in neurological disorders and
diseases. He got her in there and, believe it or not, her life
improved shortly after getting there."

"Sally, I am so sorry I ever questioned your motive. I
mean, I didn't mean to. It's just that, well, um—"

"Stop stammering already, OK?"

"OK, I will, but there's more, isn't there?"

"My dad?"

"Yeah, what happened to him?"

"The year after my mother died, my dad suffered a massive stroke while driving the rig on the Mass Pike. He crashed into the guardrail, the truck jackknifed, rolled over, and he was pinned under the steering wheel. It took the jaws of life to pull him out of the truck. By that time, he had lost so much oxygen to the brain that paralysis set in by the time the ambulance arrived. He was in the acute care hospital for almost two months between the injuries he sustained and the effects from the stroke. They sent him to a step-down rehab hospital, but Medicare paid for only fourteen days. That's when it all started. They told me at the rehab hospital that he needed to go to a 'rehab facility.' They *never* told me it was a nursing facility. I asked what was wrong with this *rehab facility*. The social worker explained that a rehab facility is where a stroke patient like my father goes for intense rehab—physical therapy and occupational therapy—to prepare for going home. The point is for the person to stay long term and guarantee another full bed for the nursing home to bill the government at a max!"

"That's a little harsh, Sally. You mean the nursing homes only take people who need rehab to try and acquire a long-term patient?"

"You learn fast, Graham!" Sally retorted. "Yes, it's all about 'heads in beds' as some crude nursing home operators like to call their census. Too much in and out hurts their bottom line. They need the rehab patients to convert to long-term residents. It's pretty simple."

"But I *am* missing something, because I am not sure how they stay long term if they're recovering from a short-term issue like a stroke."

"That part is when I come in and almost always jeopardize my having a job! If I am not on top of getting a short-term rehab patient home in ninety days or less, trust me, inertia sets in, and it becomes harder and harder to get them to go home, and worse, to get the family to take them home or to commit to taking care of their parent in the parent's own home! I try to kill the business model of keeping them there. I am determined to get them home."

Chapter 22: Remembrances

Sally was sitting in the yard when her cell phone rang. Lately, she had been thinking a lot about the so-called "life survey." She had been supportive of Graham and his need to understand the choices people make. In fact, Sally had always been at the end zone of the decisions people make. She helped them get through the next steps that you face after your decisions, but she had to admit that she hadn't spent the time figuring out how the heck people made the decisions they made. Here was this guy who was so affected by his grandmother's death and life, and how it was reduced to living in a nursing facility, that he chose to volunteer at a nursing home and eventually quit his lucrative IT job to complete this study. There was something attractive about all of this, and she surely thought of herself as a little nuts for paying attention to this guy and actually starting to find him attractive. Being a married woman was not a deterrent to these burgeoning feelings, because her motives were pure. She convinced herself of this anyway. Sally said to herself, "We all do this, huh?"

"Hello."

"Sally, this is Graham. I have a thought about something for the nursing home and need to run it by you."

"I'm not the administrator, merely a social worker, but I'm all ears, dear."

Graham was slightly nonplussed by the "dear" part but tried not to show it. "Um, well, I want to remember them.

And, well, we need to have a remembrance ceremony. Sort of a memorial, but focused on their stories so we can remember who they were."

"So a remembrance is just another form of a memorial service? I mean, I just never heard of it called a *remembrance service* before."

"So other than being caught up in the syntax or the nomenclature, you are cool with this?"

"Graham, I am so sorry that I am not expressing myself clearly. Of course I am. I was just trying to understand exactly what you were talking about. Yes."

"Yes what, Sal?"

"Yes, I'm in. What can I do?"

"Everything, actually. Thank you in advance. You're the best. I think I, um, oh, never mind. OK, here's what we need . . ."

Over the next few weeks, Sally and Graham put together the memorial service for the people who had resided at St. Matthew over the past few years. They found a priest from the local parish, a minister from the nearby Lutheran church, and a rabbi for the few people of Jewish faith who had chosen to live at St. Matthew's.

After much discussion, they decided to call family members of the deceased. Some families had no idea why they would want to remember their loved one again so many months or even years after their death and original funeral. Graham was especially emphatic that it was not a funeral but simply a remembrance; it was not even to be thought of as a memorial service. A couple of families accused Sally and Graham of assuming they—the family members—did not ensure a proper funeral was planned and executed.

Sally thought it was an interesting exercise to see the reactions of people who so seldom visited their so-called loved ones and never attended their care plan meetings but suddenly had an interest in someone else's plans to honor them. Sally was actually asked, "Why are you even doing this?" and "Don't you think we thought to have a goddamned funeral, and don't you remember that *you* people were invited to attend?"

No, this would not be easy. Sally guessed it should be filed under "no good deed goes unpunished."

Graham went about the task of inviting his family. His mom and dad were nonplussed by the invite and Graham's rationale for doing this. They still hadn't wrapped their minds around his desire to volunteer at a nursing home for the past two years, but this was really stretching things now. Much like the other families, they inquired into why these people needed a second funeral. Graham did his best to explain that he and Sally thought they had a less than stellar life at St. Matthew's, and this was a way to celebrate their life and remember them as a person, and not just someone who slowly rotted away in a narrow little bed.

They finally agreed to come if Graham promised not to say anything that would implicate them as bad children to an elder or as uncaring, self-centered adult children. Graham readily agreed, and the remembrance ceremony was off and running. The next order of the day was to get buy-in or, actually, an approval from the administrator. Mr. Thompson was pretty easygoing about it and thought it would be a good marketing tool. Graham didn't care. He'd take his approvals any way he could get them.

Sally wholeheartedly took on the task of sending out invitations. Graham picked out readings and solicited volunteers to read and sing. He decided he would give a talk about what the residents' lives were like while they lived at St. Matthew's. He wouldn't just talk about the person's glory days from when they shone through their middle-age accomplishments. He would focus on the part of their lives for which their families were less and less present, and less aware of how their life actually transpired—the nursing home years. He would talk about the person who hid behind dementia's mask and occasionally surfaced with a remark tying him or her to their past self. He would talk about the person whom he grew to love and cherish and for whom staff toiled five and six shifts each week to keep them safe, healthy, and engaged. They would celebrate the end of their life for once too.

Chapter 23: The Remembrance Day

Maybe seventeen or eighteen people gathered on that rainy night in May. Graham's parents did not show, nor did Doris's husband or Frannie's children. George's sister was there, and Rita's widower. There were others whom Sally didn't recognize.

Sally wanted to cry, but Graham insisted this was just a start and people would be arriving late anyway "considering the rain and all."

"It's just that we put so much time and energy into this, and we were determined to make sure their families knew we cared."

"Sally, who are we really trying to convince that we cared about them as people and not just a number in our census?"

"I know, Graham, but this was supposed to mean so much more to families who never thought we cared enough for their family member."

Graham looked around the room and was quite sure neither his parents nor his aunts and uncles had bothered to come. He wasn't sure if he was hurt or could easily chalk it up to being par for the course, but he was ready and told Sally as much. "Let's start this thing."

Graham approached the podium in the dining room, where he had set up a microphone, and shuffled some papers. After those gathered saw that he had signaled the start, they settled into their chairs.

Graham suddenly feared he would lose his voice, but it happened—the words came out. As they started flowing, he noticed the room was filling up with others from the home. Some of the dietary aides from the kitchen filed into the room, as did Joe Griffin, the day cook. Flo even appeared and took a seat in the back. Then, Peggy from admissions appeared. He suddenly felt his family *was* here and knew he could start.

"I know that we, as families, come here today with mixed emotions. I am a family member, too. And I joined St. Matthew's family because I care about the people here, and I had a grandmother who lived here until the day she died. I am here for her and to honor her life—in its totality—not just her pre-nursing home years. Her life was a continuum that had a final chapter at this fine home for persons who need many hours each day of nursing care. That's all.'" Graham allowed for a dramatic pause. "I can't focus anymore on my own guilt that I wasn't here to provide care for her, nor can I spend another minute being angry at my parents for not figuring out how she could have lived at her home longer, or at least, in their home. I have processed all that. It is what it is. That's not double-speak, it's just the truth. We all go through it, but I had the unique opportunity to live out my guilt and anger by volunteering here. I learned a good deal about nursing home care and the people who don't get paid much to care for our loved ones through their dying day. I learned they had a better life at the end than we thought they did. I know, I know what you may be thinking, but I ask you," as Graham looked right at Flo, "have you ever seen how Flo interacts with the residents here—when they have had an accident, or drool, or are choking as they take their medicine? Flo is there to ensure they're cleaned and have some dignity. Flo wipes up the drool and ensures he or she doesn't choke. OK, I am here to pay tribute to the deceased, but I can't do that without giving tribute to their life and their living years. I implore you to do the same."

"I want to take a minute to play a song for you." Graham bent down and hit the play button on a little portable CD player and on came Bette Midler, singing "Hello in There" from *The Divine Miss M* album.

With quizzical looks on their faces, they listened to this song about a couple whose son was lost in the Korean War. Then came the part of the song Graham wanted them to hear. Bette sang, "Say hello in there, hello." The woman in the song is an elder with no one left, and she seems to be disappearing into oblivion as people around her don't even see there is a person beneath the watery eyes and wrinkled skin. The song's author is imploring listeners to take time to look into an elder's eyes and demonstrate to them they are still a person people care enough about to at least say hello to. Graham continued with his lesson, "This song always moved me, but I was never sure why. She could easily be singing about your loved ones whom we are here to remember today. The people upstairs at this very moment are the woman in this song. They are people, these elders, whom many eastern cultures revere, but too often in America we let them slip away from us. We can no longer provide the appropriate care and cannot leave our jobs to be there during the day with them. I can't tell you how many times I have seen staff, visitors, or medical providers walk right down the corridor of two south and pass many a lonely, elderly resident sitting there and not even say hello. I know it seems like I'm preaching now, but it's why I am here today. My goal is to pay tribute to that human being you loved who was passed by, and whom many of us forgot was a beautiful person with a rich or sometimes sad and complicated history. We will never know when a person lost to the haze of dementia was the recipient of a 'Hello' how much it may have meant to them or whether it warmed their heart for one moment. Will we?"

After a pause to dry his eyes, Graham began his closing. "I think we all want to thank St. Matthew's Nursing Care Center for how much care they provided our loved ones. We know it wasn't always perfect, but it was more than we were able to do or capable of doing. We want to thank our other family members, who couldn't, um, be here, for anything they did for our loved ones, even when we secretly criticized it for not being enough. How do we know what they were emotionally able to do? Or how much their schedules allowed, considering work and child care responsibilities? And you can always know that you did what you were capable of doing, and that you did the best you can do."

George's sister interrupted what might have been Graham's last thought and yelled out, "How do you know I wasn't capable of doing more for my brother? I could have. I know I could have, and I knew that every time I came here and saw him looking more and more lost and forlorn. I didn't want to upset my life and take him in. I know that now and have been trying to accept it, but your talk is trying to give us all a cop-out. Is that what you mean to do, sir? Because I don't need or deserve a cop-out or rationalization for not doing more."

"I'm sorry. I truly am. To you and anyone else here. Blaming or removing responsibility for family members was never part of my plan when writing this talk. I just know this has been incredibly hard for my family and me, and for the families I have worked with since volunteering here. I think we all did what we could do, or when we didn't, it was because as you say, we chose not to. I think Teresa from dining services has some cookies and tea for us. Let's talk more over a hot cup of tea."

George's sister looked pretty taken aback, but she led the way to the dining room next door, and the other seventeen people followed.

Doris's daughter blew out the candles on the table in front of the podium where Graham had addressed the group.

As they made their way down the hall, two ladies were sitting in their chairs trying to self-propel forward with their dangling feet shuffling along the corridor. As the people from the service all rushed past them, Millie said to Petronella,

"Look at all the people. There must have been something special here."

Petronella replied that she hadn't seen anything on the activities calendar about a Thursday night event. Then they both tried to get someone to tell them who they were and why they were here at their home on a Thursday night.

Millie asked, "Excuse me, can you tell me what this is all about?"

After a couple of the attendees ignored Millie and Petronella, a third said it was just a little family meeting. Petronella asked, "Can we go where you're going?"

No one heard them say anything. They were invisible to the people who had just spent an hour reflecting on their loved ones being people who shouldn't be ignored. Millie and Petronella were just another couple of old ladies sitting in wheelchairs, living in this nursing home. Maybe they presented well. Too well, perhaps. But as Graham passed them, he asked if they were up to a little cake and coffee.

Chapter 24: Memories

They were sitting in the courtyard on a chilly November day. Joan had a shawl tightly wrapped around her chest. It was blue and gray and one of the few articles of clothing Joan remembered bringing with her to this place. She was thinking about the past, thinking, *What is there left to think about but the past?* Joan was getting a little tired of the routine. She was pretty sure she could get by on her own and still not quite sure how she got here. She started to doze into a semiconscious state.

There was a blonde-haired little girl running through the fields. There was a brook near the fields and another girl, a beautiful brunette, no more than a year older, or perhaps she was the same age, playing in the brook barefoot. She was trying to catch minnows in her bare hands. While doing this, the brunette was catching mud and, even worse, slugs were attaching themselves to her legs and wrists. Joan, who must have been the blonde-haired girl, kept yelling out to the other girl to stop. The other girl wasn't listening or was just too determined to do anything but discontinue.

There was a flurry of activity when Joan got home. The other girl, who now appeared to be her sister, was in bed, and a doctor was standing over her, wrapping bandages around her wrists and legs. The next moment the girl was gone. Joan was crying and begging her mother for more information regarding where she went and what was wrong. It seemed that the sister was sent to the local hospital.

The other girl spent weeks in the hospital's chronic conditions ward. The doctors determined that the slugs had poisoned her bloodstream and caused permanent damage to her central nervous system. Jennie Barbach, at the age of seven, was now "crippled," or so the doctors and her parents declared back in 1929, per the vernacular of the time.

Her parents decided they couldn't manage a girl who needed a wheelchair in their home. Jennie was sent to a state school for disturbed and mentally retarded children. Just like that, she was no longer allowed to live like a normal little girl her age.

Her life became a living hell. It was a hell that didn't include physical therapy and even minimal nursing care, with hardly any tenderness or anything that remotely resembled loving care. Ten years almost to the day, Jennie turned seventeen and declared herself an emancipated minor.

She had seen *Gone With the Wind* one night at the school, which was a rare pleasure. Jennie was struck by the strength of Miss Melanie Hamilton. She wanted to know everything about this woman who portrayed Melanie so well. Jennie went to the school library and discovered that Olivia de Havilland was the real person behind Melanie Hamilton Wilkes. She studied everything she could get her hands on about Miss de Havilland. As she embarked on her new life, it was an easy choice for Jennie when she changed her name to

Olivia and left the state school for good. That day, Jennie/Olivia declared she would never be institutionalized again. She wanted to be free from oppression and doctors and nurses telling her she was an invalid or a cripple. After finding a doctor who provided physical therapy for her legs, Olivia began ambulating fairly well, using Canadian crutches within a year. She found a job doing piecework in a factory on Washington Street in downtown Boston. Olivia met and married a man from the factory, bore and raised three children in the Boston suburbs, and enjoyed a pretty nice life with friends and family, attending christenings, weddings, and an occasional funeral. Best of all, Olivia's live culminated in the gift of her children giving her eight grandchildren to enjoy throughout the autumn and winter of her life.

It was a Saturday in April of 2005 when Olivia's granddaughter, Molly, was getting married at a country club down in Kingston, Massachusetts, not far from the pilgrim's landing in Plymouth. Olivia was so excited! As an eighty-three-year-old widow with not much to get excited about anymore, it was easy to understand why this was the event of the year for this woman. Olivia hadn't been able to give her three children much in the way of fancy weddings. She contributed what she could to Elks and VFW hall weddings, and her daughters were fine with what she could give. Olivia's son married into a working class family, and his bride was the sixth of seven children, so his was also a fairly inexpensive wedding. Jack had done pretty well, working his way through college and landing a great job in sales for a plastics company. He provided well for his three children and was proud as a peacock to be giving his daughter, Molly, away in Boston's Cathedral of the Holy Cross, directly across the street from the factory where his mother and father met and fell in love. It was now a condominium building with a mortgage company on the street level. Still, he was very proud of his humble beginnings and how his son, Jack, would escort his grandmother up the aisle of this cathedral in her blue taffeta grandmother-of-the-bride dress up to the front row of this beautiful old piece of Boston history.

It was a beautiful wedding. Olivia would always remember the flowers and Molly's dress, but not much else. On the way to the reception, Olivia asked her son where they were going and why it was taking so long.

"Oh, Mother, we're going to the country club in Kingston. It's only a couple of towns from where we live."

"Then, why aren't we there yet?" Olivia asked innocently.

"Because, silly, we left from the church, not our house. Are you joshing me?"

"Oh, of course, dear."

Another ten minutes went by and traffic on the Southeast Expressway was piled up as usual for this main artery that takes folks from Boston to the south towns. Again, Olivia asked where they were and where they were going. Her son, Jack, knew his mother occasionally forgot a detail or someone's anniversary or birthday, but "don't we all?" was how he typically chalked it up. His mind was on the bill at the country club, his daughter's happiness, and his son staying away from the bar since he was only nineteen. So this just wasn't grabbing Jack's attention, but he did continually remind his mother that this is Boston traffic—a seven-day-a-week affair that he wasn't too fond of either—and to just stop worrying about it.

"But, Jack, the church is walking distance from your house."

"Mother, you know Molly got married in downtown Boston at the cathedral. She didn't get married at St. Mary's!" He was sounding a little more annoyed than he meant to sound.

"Yes, of course, dear. I am so sorry I'm being such a bother to you today. You look so handsome and seem so proud. I would be too if I had a daughter like Molly and had the means to give her a home like you did, and a wedding at the cathedral. I know I didn't give you much, but I did the best I could. I *am* sorry, honey."

"Oh, Ma, please stop. I couldn't have asked for anything better than what you gave me and I—"

Olivia had begun crying and was suddenly wailing. Her shoulders were convulsing and her brow was sweating.

"Ma, what's wrong? Do you need a doctor? If so, Dr. Emerich will be at the reception."

"I don't know. I just don't know what's wrong. Everything is wrong because everything is so confusing. I don't know

where we are going and where I am. I don't know who I am,
I, I, stop—"

"Ma, we *are* getting you to a hospital now."

"No, please. Just leave me alone."

"But you're not feeling well, Ma. We'll take care of you."

They drove to the nearest hospital. After a full check-up
and a couple of sedatives, the attending on duty insisted she
stay the night for observation. He also insisted Jack and his
wife, Joanne, go to their daughter's wedding. They did. It
may have felt like the right thing at the time for their daughter's sake, but it wasn't the right thing for their mother and
mother-in-law. Abandonment issues can come back with a
vengeance, and they did. Olivia experienced something akin
to a "breakdown" at the Quincy Hospital. Not necessarily
because her son wasn't by her side, but because the onset
of dementia had been creeping up on her body and mind
without enough warning. Well, not enough warning signs to
which anyone paid attention.

Olivia had done the usual misplacing of car keys, neglect-
ing the stove while dinner was in the frying pan, and leaving the tub water running until it started to overflow. But
when you're widowed and live alone, who's going to notice
that? When you're in total denial that something might be
wrong with you, who are you going to tell that you almost
flooded your apartment or burned down your kitchen? You
don't. Olivia didn't, anyway. Or perhaps you're not in denial

but just have no idea that your body and mind are going through a degenerative transition. Olivia had started looking in the mirror and asking Jennie where she had been. This was occurring more frequently, unbeknownst to anyone. No one heard any of those questions posed to a mirror. No hidden cameras or microphones were in her lonely apartment or there might have been a neurological work-up or a trip to the nearest psychologist.

So began a long day's journey into night at the Quincy Hospital, a nightmare from which Olivia would never recover. During the night, Olivia screamed for help and begged to go back home. When she asked the not so unreasonable question pertaining to where she was, the nurses wrote in their shift notes, "Demented patient not oriented to place or time."

This entire evening and the nurses' treatment of her really agitated Olivia. By 2 a.m. she leapt from bed and walked out to the hall toward the nursing station to ask again; the nurse on duty walked her back to bed and then wrote, "Demented patient in 507 wandering hallways—need to refer to social services for a nursing home placement." By 3 a.m., when Olivia woke from a semi-sleep and yelled "Where is Jennie?", the prolific nurse came into the room and asked the patient in 507, "Ma'am, who is Jennie?"

"I am. Who are you?"

"Ma'am, your name is Olivia."

"I'm Jennie. And please leave me alone."

Prolific nurse went back to her station to add to her notes, "Patient in 507 is delusional and is not oriented to person or herself; need nursing home placement as soon as possible."

The next day, the social worker from the social services department came to meet Olivia. After a pleasant interview with an exhausted Olivia, the social worker wrote in her notes that "Mrs. Olivia O'Brien is a pleasant 79 y.o. woman with early to mid-stage dementia. Ambulation normal. Other than typical age-related issues, good overall physical health. I recommend an Adult Day Program 5x week with a referral to inter-faith volunteers for a friendly visitor on weekends or evening when family not available, will need informal supports from family for 'uncovered times.' Patient states there is a son and grandchildren in adjacent town."

The unit manager met with the social worker, reviewed her recommendations, and directed her to refer Olivia to at least three nursing homes. She explained that the insurance would not cover one more day for this woman without physical issues, and there was no time to set up home care services or an adult day care health program. When the social worker protested, she was told to stop being such a bleeding heart and that the nursing home would do the right thing and discharge her as soon as they arranged for these services with the family.

The social worker asked who at the nursing home was going to do all that. She was told not to be so silly, that their social worker would do all that. The hospital social worker knew most nursing homes had only one social worker for the entire house and that this, and a host of other factors, would prevent this from ever happening for Olivia O'Brien. With those few words, Olivia's fate and script were sealed.

The social worker went to Olivia's room, knocked on the door, and entered. Olivia asked where her son was and when she was going home.

"I'm sure he'll be here to visit soon."

"Well, he'll have to so I can get home. I was driving with him to the wedding, so I don't have my car."

"Oh, you have a car, Mrs. O'Brien?"

"Please call me Olivia. What do you mean, do I have a car? Of course I have a car. How else does one get around a suburb?"

"Oh, but of course. I wasn't thinking. Do you still drive at night?"

"Why, yes, I do."

"Have you been stopped at all for going too fast, or possibly too slow, or has a police officer thought you might have been drinking when you hadn't drank a drop?"

"Miss Hogan—by the way, I know that from reading your name tag—is this the Spanish Inquisition or a game of twenty questions? This shouldn't be so difficult. My car is not with me, and I do not know when my son is coming to take me home. I only ask that you tell me that."

"Mrs. O'Brien, he is going to visit you a little later, after you get settled."

"Get settled? What does that mean? I don't have to be settled in my own home. Miss, what is going on here?"

"You are having a little layover at a rehab for a week, just until everything is better again."

Stella Hogan could not believe she lied like that to a client. And so easily. She felt sick to her stomach, but furthermore she didn't understand why this woman seemed like a completely different woman than the one written about on paper by the nurse on duty the night before. And to make matters worse, she knew in her heart that this lady—this patient—should not be sent off to a nursing home. Stella did part of her Master in Social Work training at a nursing home. She knew that it was the "Hotel California"— once you check in, you never leave. Stella was especially disgusted with herself because she knew this lady had no idea she was being sent to live in a nursing home, and Stella was completely complicit in making this her new reality and life script.

"Well, Miss Hogan, I suppose if I hurt my back or whatever it is you say I hurt, then a little time at a rehab spa couldn't hurt. I could use a rest anyway. Do they have facials there? I have heard all about these spas and the gorgeous facials they give. When do I go, and how do I get there?"

"Oh, of course, honey, they have great rehab facilities there. You just wait and see how much relaxation you'll find there."

"Thanks, sweetie. I am so looking forward to it. This way I can recuperate without being a burden to my children, especially my son. He has a family of his own and doesn't need to be worrying about me. Do you know what I mean?"

"Oh, of course, Mrs. O'Brien, I know. You're independent and don't need them looking over your shoulder all the time, do you?"

"That's it, honey. Now, how are you getting me to this spa?"

"The limo is on its way now, Mrs. O'Brien."

Olivia was taken into St. Matthew's through the front door on a stretcher from the ambulance. The ambulance driver asked the front desk where he was taking Mrs. O'Brien. The receptionist asked him to wait a few minutes while she looked into it. After a harried phone call to the social worker, Sally Cournan, she yelled back to the ambulance driver to take the elevator to the third floor and take a right off the elevator to take her down to room 312. Olivia was taken into the elevator. It felt cold with just a thin sheet over her and a bag of clothes on top of her feet. She was taken to room 312, and as the ambulance driver said good-bye, she asked him what happens next.

"I'm not sure, ma'am, but I think one of the nurses will be over soon." He hoped he was telling the truth. He could have cried, but he'd done this just a few too many times and had learned how to bite his lip pretty hard to keep it in. He looked back and thought about the only way Mrs. O'Brien would leave this place—on a similar stretcher, but owned by the funeral director and taken out the back door to the waiting hearse.

Olivia was starting to wonder what kind of spa this was and why her son wasn't here to greet her and make sure she was fine after her hospitalization. A sudden fear poured over Olivia as she felt she no longer knew where she was, who she was, whether she had been tricked, and what the future would hold. Then it hit her like a ton of bricks. She had been in one of these to visit her neighbor many years ago. More recently, Olivia had visited her elderly neighbor at the Shady Pines Nursing Center. She *was* in a nursing home. Olivia screamed out, "Help! Somebody help me! There's been a mistake, and I don't belong here. Somebody help me!"

Flo came running down the hall and found her new resident in 312 in a fearful rage.

"Mrs. O'Brien, I was just on my way to admit you. I am so sorry if I'm a little late. What seems to be the matter, dear?"

"How do you know my name, and what does 'admit me' mean? Is this a spa for rest and rehab, or have I been tricked into going to a nursing home?" Flo knew what had happened and guessed which hospital referred this poor woman to St. Matthew's. She had read this chapter of the book before and knew how to approach this.

"Why, it's a little of both, ma'am. This is a place where you can relax and get some rehab. If your joints are sore, we've got a very good physical therapist to help out. If you want your hair done, we have a beauty parlor on the first floor. It's open Tuesday and Thursday until two o'clock. And yes, this is a residence where we have nurses like myself available 24 hours per day in case anything happens to anyone living here." She couldn't have been any more perky in her delivery, a rare feat for Flo.

Olivia already seemed less panicked but couldn't help picking up on the operative word "living" in Flo's last sentence. She quieted down and feigned understanding so Flo would go away. Olivia began hatching an escape plan. She would wait until dark and get dressed in her nice clothes, then slip out a side stairwell. There would have to be an emergency door or back door somewhere near the bottom of the staircase. She would get outside, find the main street, hail a cab, and get the cabbie to take her back home. She imagined saying 1525 Wood . . . then she didn't know how to finish. Wood what? She surely didn't forget her address. She lived on Woodside, no it's Woodmere, no it must be Woodward. Frustrated, she stopped imagining her plan and thought about food. Woodbridge never did cross her mind; neither did the fact her once very sharp mind was slowly deteriorating. No one who is going through the advent of dementia is necessarily able to comprehend that. This would take some sort of out-of-body experience, to look down at oneself and observe the behaviors, speech patterns, the dialogue with others. Olivia knew, though, that something was not right and again held back tears.

Chapter 25: A Reunion

The following day, Olivia was escorted a level down to the activities room. They were going to play a game of trivia. Olivia looked around the room at all these elderly folks. Many were in their wheelchairs, others had their walker parked by their seat, others were sitting around round tables staring off into space. One poor soul, Olivia observed, was drooling. Olivia handed her a napkin that she noticed on the table. The lady smiled at Olivia and nodded a sign of gratitude. Olivia wanted to cry for these poor souls.

Joan Hamilton, a lady with brown hair streaked with only a little bit of gray, looked sharply at Olivia; she almost stared but then turned away when she feared she was being rude. Whenever Joan could sneak a peek, she would peer over at this new lady and stare at her eyes and facial features. Joan then asked the activities director if she knew the new lady's name. When she replied that she didn't know, Joan asked her to ask the lady if her name was Jennie.

"Excuse me, ma'am, welcome to the activities room. My friend, Mrs. Hamilton, thinks she remembers you. Might your name be Jennie?"

"No, I'm Olivia. I don't know who Jennie is, but my name is Olivia O'Brien, and the poor soul must be confused."

"I'm so sorry to have bothered you. It happens all the time. We remember someone from long ago whom we haven't seen in years, and then a stranger walks in and reminds us of that person. Anyway, glad you're here. Did you just join us at St. Matthew?"

Olivia looked enraged. "Join you? I was brought here against my will and don't intend to stay long. Once my son gets here, he will get me home as soon as possible. I've done all the resting I intend to do. Thank you very much, Missie."

"It's Joan. Joan Hamilton, not Missie."

"Oh, you know, I had a sister Joan, but I haven't seen her in many years. I imagine she could be dead."

"Why didn't you stay in touch? I'm sorry, I know that's awfully personal for having just met you."

"Well, you know, Miss Hamilton, I don't know which way is up these past few days, so I couldn't even begin to tell you what happened, but I know we were split apart when we were very young. I miss her to this day."

"I feel that way about my son and daughter-in-law, Miss O'Brien. I still don't know why they brought me here. It's not that I haven't gotten used to it, because I have. And, I *do* like the staff. But what was I saying—"

"That you don't know why they brought you here. I know, because I think my son did this by mistake, Joan."

"Oh, yes. I tried so hard to help around the house when they were at work during the day. I made my bed, I tried to do the ironing. The laundry I couldn't do because it was located down in the basement, and they didn't want me falling down those steep cellar steps. I used to take walks around the neighborhood to stave off the boredom. Those streets all look the same, you know. So I would—as you would too, I'm sure—get a little confused and lost. A couple of times the police came to help me find my son's home. I was so embarrassed. I don't know for sure but have always hoped this wasn't what caused them to dump me here."

"Olivia, no son in his right mind would dump his lovely mother into a nursing home. You must have sat and discussed it together."

"I guess that's the question. I have no recollection of discussing any such thing. I would never allow the conversation to go on that long."

This continued for hours that day, and the next day, and the week after. Joan and Olivia adored each other and couldn't get enough time together. They even asked Sally Cournan if they could switch their current roommates so they could room together. Joan helped Olivia through the transition to life in a nursing facility more than any staff or even Olivia's own family. There was a mutual trust that was immediately apparent. Joan and Olivia could both be characterized as having most signs and symptoms of early to mid-stage dementia. Each one could gaze off and lose their train of thought, yet each one had enough short-term memory to know they found the other intriguing. Joan told stories about her previous life in the community and how she perceived her transition to St. Matthew's transpired. She talked about being tricked into going for a ride and arriving at the nursing home and being told it was a rehab center. Olivia immediately injected stories from her recent tricking and exclaimed that she was told it was a spa. They agreed they had wonderful sons one day and decided the next day their sons were nasty creatures who didn't care about their own mothers.

A few weeks later, on Mother's Day, the Hamilton and O'Brien sons had both come to St. Matthew's to do their "Mother's Day duty" and see their mothers in their respective nursing home residences. When Luke Hamilton walked into the activities room to look for his mother, he walked right toward the back of the room where his mother usually sat and approached her wheelchair from behind to rest a hand on her shoulder and give her a kiss on her cheek. Olivia turned her head to say hello to her son and shrieked loudly, "WHAT DID YOU DO TO YOUR HAIR! Wait, who the hell are you?"

"Oh, Mother, it's me! What's wrong?"

"What's wrong? A strange man comes over and kisses me, and I am supposed to just accept it? What do you think is wrong? Just because I live in a place like this hellhole does *not* mean I am suddenly cheap and easy! Do you hear me, mister?"

"Mother, it's Luke, don't you know me? I'm your son. I love you and care about you and I . . . I come here almost every day." He paused to catch his breath and quietly, as if to himself, added, "Are you slipping away from me?"

Olivia heard him. "Slipping away from you—are you kidding? I don't even know you. How could I slip away from you? Will somebody get this crazy man away from me, please!"

Luke was both scared and sad. He decided this dementia or Alzheimer's, or whatever it was, seemed to be taking over his mother's heart, brain, and soul. He had an epiphany that helped him to understand, or rationalize anyway, that he did the right thing in sending his mother to this nursing home. He wasn't doing anything in vain and wasn't selfish by giving in to his wife's wishes; he truly sent a woman on the brink of brain and body functioning with this dementia into the right and best setting—a nursing home where nurses, doctors, and Alzheimer's specialists would take great care of her. He suddenly felt the weight of the guilt—at least a 200-pound barrel's worth—wash away from him.

He said again, "Mother, I am so very sorry for all the hurt you believe I have caused you, but please don't forget me. I love you, and I want you to remember all our good times we had together."

"I don't forget those good times, dear. Don't worry. And please get your mind checked for memory loss. I have to worry about my own son not knowing who his mother is," Olivia said as she wheeled herself from the adjacent table to Joan's table.

"You know this man?" Olivia asked.

Joan answered, "Why sure, Olivia, he's my son, Luke."

Luke took a few minutes to digest the fact that he approached the wrong woman in a wheelchair at St. Matthew's Nursing Home. He mistook his own mother. One of the CNAs told Luke not to worry as it happened all the time.

She said that staff had confused the two of them often since Mrs. O'Brien arrived a few weeks ago. Luke asked her if she knew where Mrs. O'Brien came from. She wasn't much help in her response. So Luke approached her later that day with an apology for startling her. She had already forgotten the incident, but it gave him a chance to look into her eyes.

When Luke walked to his car, he couldn't get Olivia O'Brien and her hazel eyes out of his mind. They were so similar to his mother's dark green eyes. After much thought, he was determined they must be distant cousins or something like that. He was going to ask about her family and find out whether they were some relation or not. Now that made sense, especially if she was also from Boston. Maybe her maiden name was German as well? Joan Hamilton was once Joan Barbach. Luke pondered what this was all about.

Later that week, Luke returned to St. Matthew's and asked Joan if she remembered distant family, like a second cousin, from another part of the country or state.

"Well, dear, I know that my mother's family, the Ziegler cousins, moved to Michigan. And most of the Barbachs had moved to Buffalo. My parents were some of the only ones in the family who stayed in the Boston area. Why do you ask?"

"I just thought it was strange that you didn't seem to have any family. No brothers or sisters or cousins. So I, in turn, had no cousins on your side and always wondered about it."

"Jennie." Joan said flatly.

"Jennie?" Luke asked softly but quizzically.

"Yes, Jennie. She was my retarded sister. I think she was my twin."

Luke was completely and utterly flabbergasted and couldn't decide if this was one of his mother's dementia-inflicted moments or if she was joking with him. She was looking at him strangely, and her eyes looked on the verge of tears.

"A retarded sister? Mother, what are you talking about? You have *never* told me you had a sister or about anyone in your family who had an intellectual disability. Could this be a neighbor or a friend?"

"No, Luke, Jennie *was* my sister. My parents sent her away to an institution. I think they called it a 'state school' or something like that. My parents couldn't bear to see her there, and one day they received a letter that she had died there. They didn't want to tell me, but I found the letter in my father's top bureau drawer."

"You read a letter from your father's drawer that said your sister, Jennie, had died?"

"Yes, dear."

"She didn't die, Mother."

"Oh, Luke dear. This is really affecting you. We shouldn't talk about such matters. Why don't you tell me about the kids and what they're up to. I have never talked about this and shouldn't be now. I'm really quite upset."

"Mother, you don't seem 'quite' upset. Secondly, I am not crazy. I think she is very much alive and living nearby, in fact, she may be living here. In fact, I think she is sitting at the next table. Look at Mrs. O'Brien. Take a good, long look at her."

"She does seem like a lovely woman. I do see that she bears some resemblance to me. And we have spent some time together, and I believe she likewise has German heritage." After a pause, "Luke, this isn't 'The Guiding Light' for God's sake! Besides, her name is Olivia and not Jennie. And she isn't mentally retarded like poor Jennie."

"Mom, you don't understand. Your sister was probably not mentally retarded. Back then, the state put many people who didn't show any signs of retardation into facilities. They called them state schools to allay the guilt of the parents. I remember reading about this in college. These places were known as 'dumping grounds' for children with some behavioral issues, psychological issues, or even learning disabilities. What we now know as autism was also once a reason for sending kids to these awful places, these cold institutions."

"So if my sister, Jennie, didn't really need to go there, I don't understand a couple of things. Why would my parents have sent her there, and why did the school say she died?"

"I have no idea why Grandma and Grandpa sent her there, but you have to believe they must have felt as if they were doing the right thing, or a doctor or some other respected person led them to believe this was the right thing to do. I am curious about the 'death letter.' Who knows if the letter was real or not? All I know is that Mrs. O'Brien looks exactly like you. Most of the nurses, CNAs, and activities staff have said the same thing."

"Have you ever heard of coincidence?"

"I sure have, Mother, but this is different. I feel that I *know* her. I look at her eyes and see you. You have the *exact same* eyes." At this, Joan's eyes welled up and the tears flowed mercilessly.

"I have never really mourned my sister, and now that I have this glimmer of hope, I'm mourning for my parents and the grave sins they committed."

"Let's not worry about them right now. Let's approach her. Are you ready, Mom?"

"As ready as I'll ever be." Luke wheeled his mother over to the new lady, Olivia O'Brien. Luke approached her first and asked if she had a minute to talk. Olivia seemed a bit on guard at first, as this was the crazy guy that called her "Mother" and now wanted to be friends. After giving her consent in the form of a slight nod, Luke and Joan positioned themselves in front of Mrs. O'Brien. Joan looked straight into her eyes. This more than captured Olivia's attention. Joan abruptly and sharply spoke just one word.

"Jennie!"

Olivia O'Brien looked at Joan and opened her mouth as if to shriek or perhaps cry. She simply said, "Why did you call me *that* name, and who are you anyway?"

"Luke, I told you this was all wrong, and we shouldn't have bothered this poor old woman. She's not my sister."

Luke started to respond when Mrs. O'Brien looked at his mother and spoke calmly.

"Joan." Dead silence. "I tried not to let myself believe the impossible. I had a feeling since I laid eyes on you, but thought it was my memory loss, or dementia as they seem to be calling it. Is it really you?"

"It's me, Jennie. I am Joan."

At that, they both burst into tears and hugged. Luke himself cried. He selfishly wanted to know whether he had cousins and what other secrets could be revealed, but decided to leave that to another day. At their insistence, he left to speak to Sally in social services to determine if there was any way possible—if they chose—to share a room. After more than seventy years apart, Luke assumed they were not going to spend another night separately.

Luke drove home and thought about the whole event of twin sisters meeting each other seventy years later. Throughout his drive, he thought about this and rationalized that this event would now make his mother happy at St. Matthew's; and he was glad she was there. He even managed to convince himself more than usual that maybe he did the right thing after all.

In the meantime, Joan and Jennie—who actually preferred that Joan get used to Olivia, since it's all she's known for seventy years—continued talking late into the night about their lives and what the other missed. They laughed at the irony that institutionalization tore them apart and strangely brought them back together.

Chapter 26: Transitions

It was a chilly November Wednesday afternoon when the funeral director's transport station wagon pulled into the back parking lot of St. Matthew's. Mr. Falvey's assistant, Dan Burns, got out and went inside to announce their arrival. Moments later, Peggy came to the "special back door" to let them in. Once in, they swiftly made their way up to the second floor to retrieve Rita Baker, or the body of Rita anyway.

The nurses and staff orchestrate this process carefully to "protect" the residents from seeing the stretcher carrying their dead neighbor out the back door, into the cold transport wagon, and then onto the embalmer's embalming room. What they don't seem to *get* or even notice at all is that the residents face the concept of death with a matter-of-fact attitude and approach. Maybe it's their age or the fact they had a pretty good idea when they were admitted here that this would be their last move. But no one ever questioned a death each month or more often at St. Matthew. It doesn't mean that it's necessarily pleasant to see the stretcher being rolled to the elevator with a sheet over someone that you just dined with a week or so ago. But, again, it is what it is, and they seem to have learned how to let it go.

Nonetheless, the residents are kept in their rooms or in the common areas when the stretcher makes its way to the elevator and then through the first floor hallway to the back door that leads to the transport wagon's open rear door.

There is no more Rita. No more screaming in the night to "Help me get back home!" or the accusations to Sally that her son has imprisoned her here and forced her to live here against her will. No more. Rita is at peace. Maybe in her last moments her final vision was of her home—the one where she raised her children and cooked meals for eight or nine people each night—and in this vision she sees a woman with a memory as sharp as a tack and answers for everyone who needed her. She slept in a queen-sized bed with her husband, walked into her shower off her bedroom, and then picked out and put on what she would wear to work that day. Hopefully it was a vision that helped pull Rita to the other side and enabled her to die peacefully.

The housekeeping team descended on Rita's room a little less than an hour later. They packed up her clothes in plastic bags with the imprint "Patient's Belongings" on the outside. They stripped the sheets, and the detritus of her last day was removed. The pillow was removed, but the mattress remained, without even being flipped over. New sheets were placed on the bed, and the cleaners mopped under the dresser and the bed. After they made the bed, they double-checked that there were no belongings in the dresser or closet. They found an old shoe in the closet that got tossed into the garbage barrel and a mateless sock in the back of the drawer. Rita's last few belongings did not make it into the "belongings" bag.

They landed in the trash. Rita's life in the nursing home was summed up in a small plastic bag via a twenty-five-minute process.

Peggy Taylor and Sally Cournan conferred to determine the comings and goings of the day. One guy was discharged from his "rehab stay," and Rita was dead. Two other beds were empty. The local hospital needed nursing facility availability for three discharges by 4:30 today. They could do it. Peggy had just spoken to housekeeping, and Rita's room was ready. The guy from rehab wasn't there long, and the cleaning of his room was minimal.

Peggy asked, "Sally, did you see Rita leave?"

"No. I know the Falvey Funeral Home guys were here, but by the time I got upstairs they already had her in the elevator. She was so gone—her mind had diminished pretty badly in the past three years. She didn't know who her children were anymore. It was time. It was Rita's time to move on."

"I know. It just happens so fast. I saw Rita when I left yesterday at 5:30 in the afternoon. I come in this morning and she's dead. The afternoon rolls along, and her body's gone. I never said good-bye."

"Peggy, I didn't really know you got involved with the residents. It's sweet."

"I've been here more than seventeen years, and they have become my family. My parents are both deceased, so I guess that's why. I don't really know, I guess. I do know that it's their home. They didn't exactly choose it, but it does become their home, and we become their surrogate family. Sometimes we're all they have. So, yeah, I do know why I get involved and like to see them when they're going out the back door."

"Sally, it is their home, isn't it? I can only hope people like you will be there for me when I'm suffering from dementia and am somehow searching for a familiar face and loving touch."

The new patients came in within an hour and were all admitted by five o'clock. A new batch of confused and bewildered people were being sent here today by families or hospital discharge planners. Some of these "senders" believe it will just be for short-term care, a little rehab until they can get back on their feet. Others well know that this is a long-term placement, the end of the line. These placements seem to be the result of no one else being available or willing to take them in or help provide care. In some cases, it's because no one could figure out how to arrange for the care or juggle life with the needs of an aging or frail parent.

Peggy and the three-to-eleven nurses are all ready to greet the Friday afternoon arrivals. The beds are waiting, the admissions packets ready to be brought to each arrival for their multitude of signatures required. The pat answers are ready for the questions about "How long will I be here?" and "Why was I sent here?" The nurses have all gotten pretty good at saying, "Let's wait for the doctor. He'll check you out and let us all know what your plan looks like."

Roberta, one of today's new admissions, asked, "But he's never met me. Why is he telling me how long I have to be here? How 'bout I tell him how long I'll be here? Once this hip is healed and I can do steps again, I am going back to my own home."

"Of course you will, of course you will. We can figure this out," Peggy offered.

In 2009, seventy new people were placed at St. Matthew's, and sixty-one people died there. Eight people were transitioned home after a rehab stay. One person, Olivia O'Brien, insisted on going home and with the help of a neighbor, was able to go home. The neighbor once worked for the Visiting Nurse Association and understood home care services and how to set them up. She also knew that Olivia had some money and figured that instead of writing a seven-thousand-dollar check to the nursing home each month, she could spend about that or less on some private care once the VNA's authorized services were up. Joan's family has been negotiating with the O'Brien family about how Joan could join her. Maybe this could work some day before it's too late.

The circle of life and the circle of death continue at St. Matthew's and every nursing home in this country.

CPSIA information can be obtained at www.ICGtesting.com
Printed in the USA
BVOW05s0533250914

368230BV00001B/3/P